'Brendan Nichols' powerful strategies have massively increased my success. It's put so much money in my bank account that money has become a non-issue – I am now financially free! My lifestyle is now truly amazing and I am living the life of my dreams. Brendan's information is awesome!'
Ross Mclean, Director, Neptune Products

'Just one idea from Brendan Nichols led to an additional 1.1 million dollars profit within that calendar year'
Tony McChesney, Director, Compaction Australia

'The work I have done with you has significantly impacted my life, my relationships and my financial success. I run two highly successful businesses and now live in my dream home, an 8-acre waterfront property on a large lake. I have what I consider an extraordinary life. Many thanks for your contribution and great work.'
Jeff Muir, Author

'Brendan Nichols' brilliance has put serious money in my bank account. His strategies and techniques have taken my business from a $0 income to $300,000 p.a. in 18 months. I only wish I had discovered him sooner. He is remarkable at cutting straight to the central issue of what needs to be done and providing a winning formula. What is even more remarkable is that these formulas are low cost but bring big returns.'
Andrew Coldbeck, Director, The Job Shop Australia

'In just a few short months Brendan Nichols took us from a struggling business to an extraordinary success. His brilliant strategies produced sold out shows, time after time. Our business has literally taken off and our profits have dramatically escalated. If you want someone who knows the fast track to success, he is the guy.'
Pia Almarker, Almarker Designs, VIC, Australia

'I generated an extra $148,000 in just 12 weeks after attending a seminar with Brendan Nichols. His extraordinary information has created a total

breakthrough in my financial future.'
Martin Urban, Solutions Landscaping, Auckland, New Zealand

'Brendan Nichols Maverick Marketing tools work! At 23 years of age and running my first show, I didn't have the money to do expensive advertising. I used the exact techniques he described to generate $9,400 worth of free publicity, radio spots, advertising, local directory publications and newspaper articles. I was incredibly happy with the result.'
Daniel Fenech, Sydney

'Brendan's coaching has made a big difference in my business. In the first month of coaching with him, I brought in over $19,000 of extra sales!'
Wayne McDonald, CEO, Key Advantage, Adelaide, Australia

'Brendan Nichols Inner Circle Coaching program has been a massive support in our business success. The extraordinary tips and techniques that I have received have dramatically increased our profits and success. The last two months have seen profits exceeding $20,000 for each month. The program keeps me on the right path of constantly developing my self, and doesn't let me slip back into following the crowd.'
Richard Denny, Director, Onsite Experts, Sydney, Australia (23 years old).

'I wish I had met Brendan six years earlier as he would have saved my business $75,000 and more importantly, saved me three frustrating years of poor results followed by another three years, of seven day per week work and study to learn how to undo all the mistakes I had made following 'conventional business wisdom'.. I know Brendan's strategies work, as they have worked beautifully for me. Don't wait six years like I did to find the real answers of how to take your business to the next level. Life's too short for that. If you are around 40 like me you have around 2000 weeks left. Don't waste another minute. Plus Brendan gave me some great ideas on how I can add value to my old business so I can sell it for a $27,000 premium more than I thought it was worth.'
Peter Stone, Director, Peak Performance Pty Ltd

The testimonials above are not necessarily typical of every single person who uses the information; results may vary from person to person.

HOW TO BE
RICH
WORKING
2 DAYS A WEEK

HOW TO BE RICH WORKING
2 DAYS A WEEK

BRENDAN NICHOLS

PUBLISHED BY
BRENDAN NICHOLS EVENTS

Published by Brendan Nichols Events
Email: info@brendannichols.com

Printed and bound in Australia by Griffin Press
Internal Book Design Claire Edwards

National Library of Australia
Cataloguing-in-Publication data: 15474

Nichols, Brendan
How to be Rich Working 2 Days A Week

1st Edition
ISBN: 978-0-646-49429-6 (pbk)

1. Success in Business 2. Finance, Personal 3. Entrepreneurship
3. Success – Psychological aspects 4. Quality of life 5. Self – actualisation

650.1

CONTENTS

DOWNLOAD YOUR 5 FREE GIFTS Worth $842 at www.RichesFromBusiness.com/FreeGift

A Great Opportunity to the readers of this book…

1: **"The 7 Steps To Increase Your Wealth and Multiply Your Income".** A groundbreaking audio program that is literally PACKED with vital information and specific techniques on lifting the lid on your income ceiling. Normally this would be $95 – yours for free as a reader of this book.

2: **PLUS – A $700 discount Coupon to Brendan Nichols "The Entrepreneur's Million Dollar Secrets" Boot Camp.** This powerful 2 day seminar has literally made past participants millions and millions of dollars.
   - The mistakes that the vast majority of entrepreneurs do that literally flushes money down the toilet and HOW TO PREVENT IT.
   - The essential steps you must use to make more money but actually work less hours!
   - The Scientific, Low Cost strategies that produce large cash profits.

3: **PLUS – "3 Reasons People Sabotage Their Success (that very few people know about) and How to Change It".** Your mindset is vital to your success. These Powerful Secrets show you why people destroy their success. Don't fall victim to being blind-sided by a Mack truck. This mini e-book will show you how to bypass these hidden mine fields and program yourself for success. Value $47.00

4: **PLUS another extra bonus – "The Financial Rescue Package" e - book.** Financial Rescue is written for people who want to get out of debt and create financial success! This powerful book covers the 5 important areas that you must know to create financial success. These 5 essential areas are the foundation that is used by every successful person. It also gives you 10 very effective tips to help you on the path to financial freedom.

5: **PLUS another extra bonus - "Create a Stampede of New Business and Profits".** The 10 rules of the successful entrepreneur. A powerful 10 day course on discovering the tools to turn yourself into a highly successful entrepreneur.

Go Now to www.RichesFromBusiness.com/FreeGift to download your free gifts.

Acknowledgements

To my wonderful family to whom I am immensely grateful. To Karen McCreadie for her help in developing the book, thank you for your tremendous commitment to excellence. To Dale Beaumont, thank you for your assistance. To my great clients and online community at RichesFromBusiness.com who allow me to serve them doing something that I love.

Disclaimer

The intent of the author is only to offer information of a general nature. All information, techniques, skills and concepts contained within this publication are of the nature of general comment only, and are not in any way recommended as individual advice. The intent is to offer a variety of information to provide a wider range of choices now and in the future, recognising that we all have widely diverse circumstances and viewpoints. Should any reader choose to make use of the information contained herein, this is their decision and the author and their company and the publisher do not assume any responsibilities whatsoever under any conditions or circumstances. It is recommended that the reader obtain their own independent advice.

THE DREADED DEAD ZONE

The Dreaded Dead Zone –
Avoid It At All Costs

It was like a scary scene from a horror movie, except this was real life. I was in Sydney as part of a national tour, which involved speaking every evening in a different city around Australia about how you can make more money in your business.

I was due on stage in a few hours and was looking through some of my latest research about achieving success and decided to go for a walk to stretch my legs before getting ready. As I closed the door, I noticed it was just before five o'clock. It briefly crossed my mind that it might be busy but I left the room anyway. As I approached the train station at Wynyard I realised 'busy' didn't come close to the mayhem in progress.

I could see two of my promoters busily distributing flyers about that night's event but that wasn't what caught my attention. I was reminded of those terrible B-movie zombie horror flicks from the 1960s. I'd just stumbled into the Dead Zone – only this was real life!

Thousands of tired, disinterested, miserable-looking people filed past me. There was no life in their eyes, no conversation, no gentleness or kindness and certainly no smiles or laughter. Everyone seemed to be operating on autopilot, focused solely on getting to the couch and the remote control as quickly as possible. And this was them leaving work – I dread to think how thrilled they must have looked in the morning!

Wynyard train station is not unique. I could have been standing in any station in any town or city around the world. In fact, my work as an international speaker takes me to all corners of the globe. The Dead Zone is ironically alive and well everywhere from New York to London to Budapest and Singapore. It is made up of millions of people in jobs they hate, just going through the motions. The Dead Zone is where people feel trapped by the circumstances of their life with no hope for a better solution, where wealth and freedom are a lifetime away – nothing more than a figment of Hollywood's vivid imagination.

I have to admit I was really shocked, and I also felt a wave of genuine empathy – not just because of the old cliché about having one life and making the most of it now, but also because it doesn't have to be that way.

I know what it's like to have been there. I remember one night a long, long time ago staying in my office until 11 pm and feeling so exhausted that I literally fell asleep in my office chair. I woke up in the wee hours of the morning with a stiff back and bloodshot eyes that felt like they were hanging out of my head.

I am fortunate enough to have lived my life on my own terms for a long time now. I don't do rush hour. I conduct my business around my schedule. I'm not prepared to crawl through city traffic to get to a job I hate. I'm not interested in watching the lights turn green in front of me again, having moved only two inches as I'm on my way to a meeting with a client I neither like nor respect. There is no way I'm going to squash myself into a humid train carriage in the height of summer. I'm certainly not interested in missing my children's special moments because I'm tied up in strategy meetings or working out how to keep the bank manager at bay for another month. And what's the point of being in a relationship if the only conversation you have time or energy for is what to watch on the TV, and you can't even remember when you last went out together or shared a really good laugh! Basically I'm not interested in battling my way through life so I can reach some mystical future milestone where easy street magically opens up. My guess is neither are you or you wouldn't be reading this book.

The Dead Zone Sucks

You may well be a successful executive with a six-figure salary and a hot sports car but if you're not enjoying a fabulous lifestyle then you're no further forward than the guy who has to work two jobs to put food on the table. If instead you've taken the plunge and jumped out of the rat race to start your own business, then certainly that dream is within reach, but if you're working harder, longer and for less money then you're even crazier than your six-figure friend!

I've had three separate companies – each of them extremely successful. The first was a hugely successful project marketing company, the second was an import clothing business and the third is a training business. It took some time and I certainly had some scary moments in my first business but I finally cracked it and worked out a way to really make the business work for me. Every one of the salespeople who worked there were in the top 1% of producers in the country. In the final 18 months I was working an average of ten hours a week, for eight months of the year. The rest of the time I was driving around in my Porsche or skiing with my family in Aspen.

I got out of the Dead Zone very quickly and I've never looked back. I moved into a new business, because I wanted a challenge and I wanted to know if I could replicate some of the ideas that worked in real estate in another sector and make it successful. I could. So for many years now I have trained tens of thousands of people – teaching them how to make more money from their business, working less hours. And that means money and the freedom to enjoy it.

(I don't say any of this to boast, however, it is important I tell you this because you need to KNOW it is possible. I believe if I can do it, you can too and I have proved that by making a lot of other people very successful).

I present throughout Australia, the United States, New Zealand, Asia and China. But I'm not teaching theory, or possibility, based on something I've read in a book, I'm teaching stuff that works. I know it works because I've proven it to myself in entirely different markets and I've proven it to my clients who have seen their new knowledge transform their results and give them the lifestyle they seek. I've taken business owners who were hanging on by their fingernails to serious profit and freedom. I have taken wage earners who had nothing and shown them how to make money in less time than when they were struggling. I've assisted multi-millionaires restructure their business so they enjoy the fruits of their labour, instead of feeling trapped by their success. As I write this book, one of my businesses is making a six-figure annual profit and only takes three days of my time per month to maintain.

They call me the holiday king because I love adventure and I love my family and combining the two is sheer bliss for me. Last year, for example, I kicked the year's adventures off by taking my family skiing for a month in British Columbia, Canada. It has always been a dream of mine to ski all the major Canadian ski resorts – a fair undertaking considering there are dozens. So far we've been to six of them. In June I spent two weeks in the eastern tip of Java. It is one of the biggest jungle reserves in South East Asia and a truly incredible place. There are no roads and the only way in is by boat. I would wake up in the morning and go for a walk along the beach – only on this beach there are leopard tracks in the sand! I would have probably jumped out my skin if I'd met one, but the idea that they were roaming wild was wonderful. The jungle was teaming with life, and monkeys howled above, flitting through the massive green trees.

On holidays I have two modes – 5-star and no-star. I can play both sides of the fence and enjoy doing so, unlike a lot of successful people who need to be seen in 'all the right places'. I love the elegance of beautiful places but I also love the wild beauty of 'off-the-beaten-track' environments. I just love adventures!

While I was on my Javanese adventure, my wife and daughter were in Europe for a month, enjoying the sights of St Petersburg and visiting relatives in Finland (Annie is Finnish).

During August I went skiing for two weeks in Thredbo in Australia, enjoying private lessons with one of the national Austrian ski team instructors. In November, it was off to Vanuatu, a beautiful tropical South Pacific island for a family getaway. We stayed in a 5-star bungalow right on the beach. Waking up in the morning and looking out across an azure blue lagoon was wonderful. Just a dozen steps into the water and I could see tropical fish swimming through the coral.

In late December we went to spend Christmas as a family in one of my favourite places in the world – New Mexico. We stayed in Taos, a high desert town with cowboy overtones ringed by snowcapped mountains, where all the buildings are adobe mud brick. And yes, as you probably guessed, one of the best ski mountains in the world.

Between the major trips there have been several weekend breaks to a beautiful coastal village in northern New South Wales. We stay in a house there that is really gorgeous; it looks onto a deserted windswept beach with bushland running right down to the ocean.

In case you are thinking I was born under a lucky star – I certainly wasn't a genius at school, far from it. I'm not trying to appear cocky or as though I'm blowing my own trumpet but seriously I live a great life and I've had no special advantages. So if I can do it so can you. Your time is precious and I need you to know – right up front – that I'm not talking a talk I don't walk. I'm not going to guarantee you a life of luxury and buckets of cash some time in the future. I'm actually going to tell you how you can have it RIGHT NOW!

So many of the business books on wealth creation written today talk about this fabulous life you're going to have … IN THE FUTURE. Offering ideas and action plans that will allow you to make a few million dollars free and clear, and then retire on the interest. Or how you should build up a huge property portfolio and live on the residual income. Forget that – tomorrow never comes. Why not enjoy the kind of life you are passionate about TODAY!

I don't agree with the 'work-yourself-into-the-ground-now-and-hope-that-one-day-you-might-have-enough-time-energy-and-money-to-enjoy-life' philosophy. What's the point of working like a dog to create a business or build a property portfolio only to find that by the time you have the money you don't have the time to enjoy it (or you're too old to ski!). Just to be clear here, I'm not advocating being frivolous with your money and spending every cent you make, but I am saying enjoy it. You need to make provisions for the long term and be financially astute, but you can do that while enjoying the here-and-now. There is only one way you can do this and it is learning how to make more money in less time so that you can live the kind of life you want right now!

My priorities in life are my relationships, my spiritual life and my financial life. The last one is only important to me in so far as it funds the other two. Money's only real power is that it gives you choice. If you were rich enough to be able to go to your local Porsche dealer and buy a brand new 911 Turbo, pay in cash and not even flinch at the cost, would you consider yourself rich?

Well, I could if I wanted to – and I'm not at the office 18 hours a day. However, here is something really interesting. Once upon a time I did own a Porsche. And to be really honest with you, a small part of the reason I owned it is because I didn't feel that good about myself. I felt better about who I was when I was in the Porsche rather than in an 'ordinary car'. These days it doesn't make that much difference to my self-esteem which car I drive. There is a lot more freedom in that. Don't get me wrong, I love beautiful things but I want to choose them for me – not for what I think someone else thinks of me.

In any year, with the holidays we take and the time I can spend relaxing at home with my family, I work a lot less than most people. I have control over how I spend my days. I'm able to watch my kids grow up and be part of their lives in a meaningful way. I haven't missed all the good bits because I've been in meetings. We're able to travel to wonderful exotic locations, to ski several times a year and buy beautiful things and enjoy some of the finer experiences life has to offer. And we're able to support the causes that are important to us and make a difference to the world in that way. Years ago one of my friends started a foundation to support children in African villages who were dying because of the lack of clean drinking water and AIDS. Money allows us to support causes that are important to us.

And all of that is possible because I have learned to make my businesses work for me, NOT the other way around. And that is what this book is all about.

I will share with you tried and tested ways to help you put more cash in your pocket today AND tomorrow. I've done this myself with my own business and I've achieved the results in several very different industry sectors – so I know it's duplicable. But don't take my word for it. Visit **www.RichesFromBusiness.com** and click on the testimonials from the people who have made a lot of money using my system.

You can make a lot of money AND have a great life right NOW! You can make changes to the way you work that will free up your time and put more money in your pocket at the same time.

Enjoying life right NOW is the only way to live otherwise you're as trapped and miserable as everyone else in the Dead Zone!

GET COMPLETELY FREE

'The 7 Steps To Increase Your Wealth and Multiply Your Income'

A groundbreaking audio program that is literally PACKED with vital information and specific techniques on lifting the lid on your income ceiling.

Normally this would be $95 – yours for free as a reader of this book.

Go now to www.RichesFromBusiness.com/FreeGift

The Snap Point – The Beginning Point of Great Riches

Everybody has a snap point. It's the point that you reach where something happens in your mind and you say 'enough is enough'. It can happen in any part of your life and from the thousands of people I've met over the years it seems to take an infinite number of forms.

For example, there's Richard Denny – who initially came to me when he first started in business. At 23 years of age he was making an average profit of $20,000 a month. Richard reached a point where he no longer wanted to be average, in fact, couldn't stand the thought of it – that was his snap point.

Or Andrew Coldbeck, another client who within 18 months went from zero income to over $300,000 profit a year. His snap point was being sick of working hard, he wanted to work smart.

Or the high income lawyer earning $830,000 income who

realised how he could make a lot more – he now makes over 2 million dollars a year and he managed to achieve this in less than 18 months. His snap point came from constantly being in the office, swamped by work. He wanted out with a raging passion.

My snap point happened in my first business. I didn't have any experience in real estate and looking back it wasn't the most sensible direction for me to take. But I was confident I'd work it out quickly enough. The real estate business had failed and the previous owner had gone broke so when I came along, full of youthful enthusiasm and not much else, the owner saw an opportunity. The business was an empty shell and the office had been closed for months. The owner suggested that I take it over and if I made it work it would be my business. I just had to pay him a percentage of the profits. Believe it or not I thought this was a good idea! It didn't occur to me that there wasn't actually a business to take over. But it gets worse … the office was three kilometres from the main shopping centre. The only other shops nearby were a newsagent, a butcher, a doctor's surgery and a couple of other small shops. There were eight car spaces and NO passing traffic. Honestly – what was I thinking?

But I was convinced that this was my lucky break. What I lacked in common sense and business experience I made up for with enthusiasm. At least, I did at the start. Before long the overdraft was up to $10,000 which back then was ALL the money in the world. The business had been open for a month and I'd been really active trying to get listings and meeting potential buyers and sellers. I'd been putting in 18-

hour days so it wasn't as though I was twiddling my thumbs. Yet I hadn't made a single sale.

I was married and we had a three-year-old daughter and I certainly felt that added pressure. It's one thing to screw up when you're on your own, but the idea of my family being destitute because I couldn't get it right devastated me. Although it was over 25 years ago, I still vividly remember sitting in the kitchen of my two-bedroom rented house in the southwest districts of Sydney. I was slumped over the old table, my elbows resting on it and my head in my hands. I felt as though I'd been hit by a truck, as the gravity of the situation I was now facing finally came home to roost.

I hadn't made a single sale and the outgoings were way more than I could cover. Just thinking about my overdraft made my eyes water. I was the sole breadwinner in the family and we had no bread. I felt ashamed. I was also really confused because I was working hard. I started looking back at what I'd done to try and find some answers and see if there was something I was missing.

I'm still not sure what actually happened but I hit the wall and I felt this rage well up inside me. I thought, 'I've had it, I'm not putting up with this anymore, I have to change something!' I'd reached my 'snap point' and there was just no way I was going to let my family down. I was working like a dog for no money and I was going to find a way to reverse the situation if it killed me.

And I did. In my mind I remember drawing a very clear distinction between my business before that point and my business after and I completely reinvented everything. I wasn't interested in the old way – it clearly didn't work and it sure as hell wasn't any fun. From my snap point on, I was only interested in making the most amount of money for the shortest amount of time with the least amount of effort. NET PROFIT was the only objective.

I began to work out a unique system that you could apply to virtually any business. From what I can see, having looked at countless businesses, less than 2% of people know this secret AND they are the ones that make the money.

I don't know if you've reached your snap point yet but if you haven't, my guess is you're pretty close. If you're currently not living the lifestyle you crave then you probably fall into the time/money trap in some form or another.

Some people feel trapped because they simply don't make enough money. Each month they struggle to meet their commitments and have perhaps even resorted to having more than one job. They have no money and no time. As a way to balance their cash shortfall, or for retail therapy, they probably have a colourful collection of credit cards. Each month they'll pay the minimum amount required and not a cent more. Even if they do realise that this tactic is financial suicide, and occasionally add a little extra to the repayment, they don't have the money to pay it all off anyway. It's better to stick their head in the sand. They are drowning in debt with no life raft in sight. It's already hard enough to service their debts, so leaving their job, setting up a business or trying to find an alternative solution is just way too hard!

Some people are lucky enough that money isn't such a problem. Or at least that's what they'd like people to think. This is the looking-good, going-nowhere trap. But it's still a trap. They've probably done really well for themselves and should be congratulated for that. They are almost certainly good at their job and their pay-cheque reflects that. But as they've moved up the corporate ladder, their tastes have changed – but luckily they've also found that access to even more money is increasingly easy. As a result their commitments have escalated beyond their income. They live in a bigger house, drive a faster car, dress in the best clothes and enjoy much more luxurious holidays. The result is much the same – they too struggle each month to meet their commitments. They may look successful, but they are expected to put in at least 12 hours a day, 6 days a week for the privilege. And even if by some good fortune or good planning their income is considerably more than their outgoings, and they do actually have money left at the end of the month, they don't have the time or energy to spend it!

This situation is often referred to as 'golden handcuffs' and if you recognise yourself then I guarantee it doesn't have to be this way. You're bright – otherwise you wouldn't be in the position where your organisation is trapping you in the system. If you haven't snapped yet, brace yourself … it's coming.

And then there are those who have taken the plunge and started their own business. That takes real courage especially when there are dependants to look after. These people deserve our respect and so if you fall into this category I salute you. And I'm also really excited for you because you've already got yourself into a position where a really fabulous lifestyle is just around the corner – where you have the money AND the time to enjoy it.

Too often business owners are working longer hours than

they did when they were employees. Too often they also make considerably less money. All they seem to do is fight fires day-in, day-out. They can't get good people, cash flow is erratic (to say the least) and the life they dreamed of when they became their own boss now seems like a pipedream. And to top it all off, they can't remember the last time they fell asleep before midnight!

Whatever your current situation, the bottom line is that if you're not happy and you're not living the lifestyle you dream of, then it needs to change RIGHT NOW! It might sound a bit odd to raise this here but I have always been acutely aware that one day I'm going to die. Not in a morbid, woe-is-me way as I'm as fit as a fiddle, but I've always appreciated that my time on this planet is limited. And I want to live it. I want to drink in all the experiences I can, I want to visit amazing places and spend time with people I love and I want to get to that day thoroughly worn out and happy. And you deserve the same.

By all means work and save for retirement and build a portfolio that creates passive income but you can ALSO live the life you dream TODAY. I'm reminded of the anonymous verse that did the rounds on email a few years back, and although I don't drink, I think it pretty much sums up how I feel …

Life should not be a journey to the grave with the intention of arriving safely in an attractive and well preserved body, but rather to skid in sideways, chocolate in one hand, champagne in the other, body thoroughly used up, totally worn out and screaming ~ WOO HOO what a ride!

The Secret to Having More Money

I'm assuming that you want more money – otherwise a book about getting rich working 2 days a week wouldn't have caught your attention! Certainly it's a common desire. I'm sure that if you were to ask one hundred people on the street what they most want, almost all of them would mention 'more money'. But money isn't a destination – it's just the fuel. What do you want money for? Once you can answer that question, you're getting closer to the truth.

For most people, freedom and money have been confused. Money can offer people freedom, but they are not inextricably linked. They don't come hand-in-hand and certainly those with money don't necessarily have freedom. I've had many clients over the years who have been referred to me because although they may be multi-millionaires they don't have any freedom to enjoy it.

This is the reason why I believe that so many people

struggle for decades to reach some magical net worth. They have confused their target destination. Somewhere in their youth they decided that 5 million dollars would be their milestone. Once they'd made 5 million dollars they would be 'rich' and would have finally arrived. (It's always a round number have you noticed? You never hear anyone wanting to make $1,769,504.) Only time ticks on, and inflation takes its toll so when they finally make 5 million dollars, it's not enough. The goal posts get moved to 10 million dollars. Then they will be properly rich and will be able to relax and smell the flowers. So they continue to work 12 hour days, their kids forget what they look like, their partner has graduated from university as a mature student and they don't even know what they're studying! They have no idea what their children's favourite subject is at school and can't remember the last time they went to watch a football game together. Then one day, they are rich – unfortunately they're also old and miserable!

Why? Because they chased money, falsely believing that money would give them freedom. Freedom was what they really wanted. Freedom means very different things to different people. But having trained thousands of people – from those with no money to those with millions of dollars – there is no doubt in my mind that people crave freedom.

My experience running seminars has taught me that there are two camps – those who want more money to move away from pain, and those that want more money so they can move toward pleasure! They are usually quite different individuals. The first just want more money so they can have more security. They're not that interested in the toys or the lavish lifestyle. Then there is the other camp – they want to be rich because of the pleasure they think it will give. They want it all – the excitement, the glamour and the luxury.

Again, this book can offer you those opportunities too. But my point is, if you break it all down, what they both have in common is – freedom! The freedom to live their life **by their own rules – whatever they may be!**

This book will give you the solutions whether you want to make so much money that you can jump in your private jet and fly to Monaco for the weekend, sail your own yacht in the Sydney to Hobart, or park it in the harbour for New Year. If you want enough money to own cars that go from 0–100 faster than it takes for your toast to pop in the morning then what I teach can and has done that.

If on the other hand, you just want to spend time with your kids and be able to buy them the things you never had, this book tells you how to do that too. If you want more freedom so you can afford to take time off and enjoy the little things in life – to play more golf with your friends or indulge your love for Thai cooking then that's also possible!

Consider the question yourself for a moment … Why do you want more money?

Why do you want a new car? Because you like the way it looks or because you love the idea that you can jump in anytime and disappear into the country? Is it the idea of driving with the roof down on an open road that's thrilling you, or being stuck in rush hour traffic on a humid summer's day? By the way, gridlocked city traffic is just as irritating in a Ferrari as it is in an Astra!

Do you want your home mortgage-free, so you can actually enjoy it without killing yourself week-in, week-out to meet the repayments? What's the point of that – you're never in the house anyway!

Do you want some extra cash in the bank so you can frame your bank statement and admire it on the living room wall during the three waking hours you spend there before collapsing into bed at night? Or is the idea that you can buy that surprise gift or fly to New York for a show without having to worry about whether it's possible or not? Do you want more money so you can work longer hours and spend more time in the office, or less?

Chances are you want more money because you want more freedom. As a starting point you would probably like to clear your personal debt, own your house without a mortgage, have enough money to do whatever you want to do and buy nice things for your family. You'd like to be able to enjoy several family holidays each year and spend more time with your friends. You'd like to laugh more and worry less. You'd like to relax knowing that your business was making money and it wasn't killing you to do it ... And after that – who knows? Once you've got the system in place to milk your business you can turn it on and off at will. It will become your own personal cash dispenser and you can go and get more whenever your want. Or you can leave it 'on' all the time and enjoy that amazing lifestyle you want – the choice is yours.

I realised long ago that money is an amazing servant but

a lousy master. Freedom was what I treasured more than anything else and if you're just as interested in the '2 days a week' part of the title as you are in the 'Get Rich' part, then you're probably the same! As far as I'm concerned money only has two purposes and that's …

'To Get a Life and Give a Life'

And I would suggest that it's exactly the same for you. Money's only purpose is to allow you to have an amazing life and help and support those you care about.

This book is about helping people who have already taken that leap of faith into business or who are considering doing so to really capitalise on that decision. Business, especially small and medium business, is the backbone of every economy. But it takes courage and determination to pull it off. Forget flogging yourself to an early grave – let's work out how to put MORE money in your pocket in LESS time than you're currently spending treading water! Let's structure your business so it doesn't exact a terrible price on your family and friends. And let's give you the freedom you deserve so you can enjoy your life right now …

GET COMPLETELY FREE

A $700 discount Coupon to Brendan Nichols

'The Entrepreneur's Million Dollar Secrets' Boot Camp

This powerful 2 day seminar has literally made past participants millions and millions of dollars.

- The mistakes that the vast majority of entrepreneurs do that literally flushes money down the toilet and HOW TO PREVENT IT.
- The essential steps you must use to make more money but actually work less hours!
- The Scientific, Low Cost strategies that produce large cash profits.

Go now to www.RichesFromBusiness.com/FreeGift

So, Seriously, How Much Do You Want?

Everyone knows about setting goals. You've probably heard of the Yale University study in 1953 where students were asked if they had written down their financial goals for the future. Only 3% of the students said they had. A follow-up survey of the same students was conducted 20 years later and it was found that the assets of the 3% who had written down their financial goals were more than the combined assets of the surviving 97% who had not.

Is that a coincidence? No, I don't think it is. The idea of goal-setting has been hijacked by the new-age personal development set and there is rarely a seminar that doesn't cover it. As a result people have become too familiar with the idea and have consequently become complacent about actually doing it.

But knowing what you want is not some namby-pamby concept. It is based on biological and scientific fact …

There is a part of the brain called the Reticular Activating System (RAS), which among other things acts as a data filtration system. The numbers vary from reference to reference, but according to popular wisdom, we are being bombarded with millions of 'bits' of information every second through the five senses. If we were consciously aware of all those bits of information we would go insane. Can you imagine being aware of every sound that's happening around you, every object in your line of vision, every sensation on your skin or everything that you brush past and every movement you make? You'd never get any sleep for a start!

So as human beings we delete the vast majority of the information. Of the millions of bits of possible information we could process, it's estimated that we actually process less than 1%! So we are deleting or not even processing over 99% of all the possible data out there.

What we delete is based on our beliefs, attitudes, values, past experiences, social expectations and conditioning. These things influence what we believe is 'normal', and probably more importantly, what we believe is possible. The RAS is the filter system that decides what we become aware of and what happily floats past.

You'll have experienced this before. Let's say you decide to buy a car and you've chosen a metallic jade MX5. You're driving your old car through the city and all of a sudden you see them everywhere. What's going on? Has a large shipment of metallic jade MX5s just descended into the city or were they given away on a breakfast radio show or something? No, as soon as you decided that you liked the MX5, your RAS filter system included that in your awareness. The cars were always there – you just didn't see them because they were not important to you. If you ask a woman who is pregnant if she has noticed that there seems to be a lot of pregnant women around, she will always agree that there appears to be an increase in pregnant women. However, it is because pregnant women are now on her radar. As a career woman with a high-powered job she noticed different things but now that she's expecting a child her radar has changed, and therefore her experience of the world around her has changed with it.

By writing goals or by knowing what it is you want out of life, you add that to the 'things to look out for' list of your RAS. Your brain then searches for information or things that are relevant to you obtaining that objective. Your internal radar system will pick up information in your environment that could be useful in connection to that outcome. So biologically it's really important to know what you're trying to achieve. Otherwise opportunities will slip past. There is a saying that states that the opportunity of a lifetime comes around every two weeks. And I totally believe that's true. It's just that most people don't see those opportunities because their RAS is not set up to look for them!

The new science of quantum physics is also illustrating that we have far more control over what happens in our lives than previously assumed. Quantum physics is basically the science of the very small. While classic Newtonian physics explains the universe very well when it comes to falling apples and spinning planets, when scientists turned their attention to the very small they found that these accepted explanations didn't work at the sub-atomic level.

Without getting overly technical, studies in quantum physics have shown that what we experience is very much influenced by what we think and feel. Studies all around the world are proving time and again that by turning our attention and focus in a particular direction we somehow influence the results toward that expectation.

One of the scientists at the forefront of this work is Professor William Tiller of Stanford University. He has conducted experiments with seasoned meditators to see if their intention could alter reality. In one experiment he got a very simple electronic box and asked the meditators to concentrate their intention on the box. The intention was to 'raise the pH of the water by 1 degree'. These boxes, along with control boxes (with no meditation directed toward the box), were then placed next to water taken from the same source. There was no change to the water in the control boxes, yet the water subjected to meditation changed in pH value. Changing pH is not an easy task and considering that a 1 degree pH rise in the human body would be fatal, the chances of this occurring naturally were millions to one.

The idea that we have much more power over what happens in our life simply by directing our intentions is not new. What is new is that science in now beginning to prove what has always been a mystical and spiritual theory.

If this new science is proving the unquestionable influence that our thoughts have on outcome, then business planning is not a necessary evil but simple common sense. If you want to get rich you need to make it a priority target and drench your mind with thoughts of wealth and how to create it. It has to become a driving intention in your world.

Part of achieving success is defining what success looks like to you. There's a great conversation between Alice and the Cheshire Cat in Alice in Wonderland. Alice wants directions and asks the cat, 'Would you tell me, please, which way I ought to go from here?' To which the cat replies, 'That depends a good deal on where you want to get to.' Alice says, 'I don't much care where.' 'Then it doesn't matter which way you go,' said the cat.

If you don't know where you're going or what you're trying to achieve then how will you know when you've arrived? You are always going somewhere; your current thoughts, actions and behaviours are plotting a course all the time. But unless you take conscious control of that process, you may end up deeply disappointed with the destination.

So before we go any further, I want you to give it some serious thought. I don't want you to put off living your dream because you think the dream is so 'far away' that getting there doesn't seem real or possible. I'm reminded of a story of a man who dreamed of owning a ranch and he worked in a job he hated saving money to allow him to buy one. He had made assumptions about how much he needed in order to buy his ranch. And eventually he saved what he thought was enough money and went off to make his dream come true. He discovered that he could have been living his dream years earlier.

You don't want to be like the would-be rancher, struggling toward some arbitrary amount based on nothing but assumption. It's important that you know what you want to achieve and are able to accurately quantify how much you will need to make in order to make your dreams a reality.

So get a nice notebook from the stationers and take some time out to describe what it is that you really want in detail. How much do you really want right now? I like to think of monthly income because it is quantifiable and you can monitor it. What you want to do is write down a figure that you make every month that is MORE than you need to have a fantastic life that month (and every month) – the rest goes in a savings or investment account.

The other alternative that is often advocated is to 'save and invest all your money for 30 miserable, no fun years, retire and then have a nice life.' Doesn't feel like much fun to me when you can have a great life now and also invest for the future. At the very least, doing this will allow your biological filter system to scan the environment and see if there is anything relevant to that goal that you need to know about so you don't miss opportunities for its attainment. And don't worry; later I am also going to give some remarkable, practical techniques about how to achieve this monthly income goal.

Exploding the Myths that Keep You Poor

Money is a strange thing. It certainly does strange things to people, but what fascinates me are all the hang-ups and misconceptions people have about it! Those that have it rarely talk about it and those that don't rarely talk of anything else!

Have you ever heard people talking negatively about money? Have you been part of those conversations? Yet the idea of talking negatively about money is as silly as talking negatively about air.

The truth is that you need air and, like it or not, you need money. This chapter is looking at the myths and misconceptions that exist about money to help clear them up for once and for all.

There is another reason this is very important. People that don't have money have lots of these misconceptions locked up in their head and people that have money don't. Big clue:

do what the people who have money do, and you are more likely to have money!

Myth 1:
If you're rich you must have done something dishonest!

There are still far too many people who genuinely believe that you have to be a ruthless bastard to succeed in business – that relentless disregard for people over profit is the only way to succeed. There is almost an unspoken understanding that those who are very wealthy must have done something dishonest to achieve such riches. Nudge, nudge, wink, wink: 'Well if you want to make an omelette you've got to crack a few eggs!' Perhaps it's easier that way. It's easier for people to criticise wealth and insinuate that it was attained through dodgy dealing than to face the fact that perhaps someone is wealthy because they don't spend five hours a night watching Friends re-runs! Maybe, just maybe, that person has money because they had a plan and were determined enough to get off their backside and make it happen!

This myth about the evil of money goes hand-in-hand with the nobility of poverty – apparently the rich are somehow immoral and the poor are not. The idea that you can be rich and a good person seems totally foreign to some people! But again, I have to question whether that's really what people think or is it just a convenient 'cop-out' for those that are simply too lazy to do anything with their life.

Whether you were born with money or not makes absolutely

no difference to your ability to make it and keep it. Oprah Winfrey is a billionaire with enormous global influence and she started her life in poverty. There are thousands of examples of those who were born poor and created amazing lives of contribution and happiness. There are also thousands of examples of those born with every privilege money could buy who wasted their opportunity and wasted their lives. Money in and of itself is meaningless – it doesn't make people good or make people bad.

I hear this all the time: 'It's immoral to have a lot of money.' What people are saying is that it is okay to have a bit of money, but not a lot. Here is my response: stealing a dollar is wrong, stealing 10 million dollars is wrong. There is no degree of 'wrongness'. Stealing something that doesn't belong to you is wrong. It's common sense. So why should having money be any different. Why is having a dollar okay and having 10 million dollars not? What makes one acceptable and the other immoral? I don't get that. You don't get more wrong depending on how much you steal, so why do you get more wrong depending on how much you legitimately make? Of course, the word legitimately is very important in that sentence. It's never right whether you're making 1 dollar or 100 million dollars to exploit or harm others in the making of that money.

Myth 2:
Do what you love and the money will follow

How many have heard that before? Is it true? I hate to

burst your bubble, but no, it's not! I really love hanging out on the beach and I just LOVE skiing. I'm really passionate about it so if I decide to do that for the rest of my life then I'll take a collection from you, wonderful reader, so that you can support me doing what I love … What do you think? Do you like the idea?

No one is going to pay you to do what you love. Trust me. It's the biggest myth in town. The only way to make money is to add value, to make someone's life better, easier or happier in some way. They'll pay you to do what you love if it serves them. That's the reality of human nature. Now don't get me wrong – you also have to love what you to do to succeed, however, just because you love it doesn't mean it's necessarily commercially viable.

People say to me all the time, 'Brendan, you know I realise the business that I'm in is wrong and I'm not passionate about it any more. I've got this new passion. I've decided that I'm going to grow cucumbers. You know I've got the most amazing cucumbers in the world and I'm going to unleash my cucumbers on the planet because everybody wants a cucumber.' But trust me, the world is not on tenterhooks waiting for your cucumbers. Most people couldn't care less about your cucumbers!

If I had a dollar for every person that had been indoctrinated with the 'Do what you love and the money will follow' BS, who were ready and willing to turn their back on a perfectly good business just because they weren't 'passionate' about it anymore, I'd be an even richer man. Whether it's a new cucumber or a blue widget, why on earth would you turn away from a viable business without testing the idea first? Am I saying that you should not be passionate about what you do? Of course not, passion is important – but just make sure it is something other people are passionate about buying.

Test it! Find out if somebody actually wants your cucumbers. Just because you're passionate about cucumbers doesn't mean anyone else will share your enthusiasm.

Let's take a step back for a second and get a reality check. No one – I don't care who they are or what they're doing – no one loves what they do ALL THE TIME. We all have to do things we don't want to – it's called 'being an adult'. I am very fortunate to love what I do, however, I have one client who I have coached and he's now very rich. He is about to sell his business for approximately 9 million dollars and I can tell you he was never in love with it. Now he wants to find what he loves and that's okay. It's also easier with 9 million dollars in the bank!

Do what you love and the money will follow is a myth that's only half true. It's popular in new-age seminars or personal development reveries, and while the idea is sound in principle, loving what you do is no sure-fire path to riches any more than hating what you do is! So by all means, explore working in areas that interest you and move your business into areas that you are passionate about BUT only if you've done the research and you know there's a market for it.

Myth 3:
You have to be really intelligent to be rich

There is a friend of mine, Mike, who is a very sharp

businessperson. Outside his office door he has a poster with a photo of John Wayne in a tough guy pose. The words on the poster read, 'Life is tough, it's tougher if you're stupid.' It's true – but not necessarily in the way most people think. First of all, being smart at school is no guarantee of becoming rich. Some of the richest people in the world were not much good at school. The kind of smarts you need are the ones they don't teach at school – the smarts that tell you the things that work in the real world and produce real-world results. And those are the things that we are going to talk about in this book. I have a lot of clients who are not overly educated, and you certainly wouldn't call them brilliant, but they follow the formula I outline and they have done extremely well. That is what I call smart: doing things that work and not just doing what the majority does. Just following the crowd is one way to pretty much guarantee a life of hard work and average results.

This is so important – especially now – and it's something that we need to be teaching our kids. The days of 'go-to-school-get-good-grades-go-to-university-and-you'll-get-a-good-job-for-life' are gone. Sure, I would encourage any kid to do well in school but beyond that I'm not so sure. Years of university, accumulating more debt than knowledge, won't always be the best route. We need to foster creativity in our kids and encourage them to think differently. The future belongs to those that can adapt and change their approach, not the ones stuck in specialisations unwilling or unable to move with the times. Careers won't last a lifetime anymore – they will be in constant metamorphosis – and those who embrace that change and the speed at which it occurs will win. Building confidence and independence so that kids have the option to conform, or not, depending on what they feel is best for them will probably be more helpful than encouraging people to fit into little boxes.

Reality: To make money you need the right vehicle

If you're going to get practical about money you've got to have a vehicle that can actually make you money. And this links back to the idea that you should do what you love and the money will follow.

Say I discover macramé and decide to start teaching seminars on macramé, how many people do you think would be willing to spend money for a weekend workshop on the joys of macramé? My guess is, that despite my enthusiastic passion for the subject (not!), I wouldn't be able to find many people to part with much money for that sort of course. The market for macramé is small and the demographic of that market are not people who would spend reasonable money on a course. You don't even have to be a marketing genius to work that out.

You've got to make sure that your money-making vehicle matches the market and it's something that people want. So right now, you need to figure out the business that you're in. Does it have the capacity to make money? Are you providing a product or service that people actually want?

Let's just say that I was living in a country town like Dubbo or Wagga Wagga, way out in the bush somewhere. I love Italian clothes and I've heard that if you follow your passion the money will follow. So if I quit my job in the bakery and open an upmarket men's clothing store, stocking Zegna and Armani plus all the latest trendy fashions, what's going to happen to the store? It's not rocket science is it? How long is it going to take before I go broke? That's not the market. The people don't want that, and if they did they would go to Sydney or Melbourne to get it.

Or let's say that I am a barber. I open up in town with a red and white pole and I'm cutting for $20, one person at a time. Even if the store's full all day and all night it's going to take me maybe 20 minutes to do a client. Add up $20 by 20 minutes and that's as good as it gets and I'm working like a dog!

You've got to understand the vehicle you have to make money and find ways to exploit your advantage to the best of your ability. So in the case of the barber shop, I may love being a barber but I'm not going to get rich doing it. Not unless I started really using the vehicle. I relaunch myself as an upmarket hairdresser, open a place in Double Bay and charge a zillion bucks for a haircut and a colour and position myself through very clever PR as the hairdressing guru … suddenly it's a whole new ball game. The vehicle has been turned into a Ferrari. And it can get even better … let's say I build a database of my customers, send them regular newsletters and build rapport. Now I have such great rapport I am able to sell other completely different products to those customers, creating whole new profit centres and all without doing a lot more work.

One of my clients, David, is a plumber who has such fantastic rapport with his clients that he is now marketing clean air purifying systems to them – all done by a simple letter that I helped design for him.

There are two questions you need to ask yourself:

Do I have the right business vehicle to make money?

Is there anyone else in your line of work that is making the sort of money you want?

Because if there is, then it can be done, and the business you're in has the potential to make you serious money too.

On the flip side, there is a word of warning. Often people get excited about the lack of competition in their sector or they are convinced that there is no one like them in the market and therefore they are onto a winner. Unless you're in some cutting edge technology company, if someone isn't already doing it there is probably a reason for that – and it's not a good reason. If there is no one else offering a $2500 macramé master class in the Hunter Valley there is probably a very good reason for that too! Ideally you want to know others are making a real success of doing what you are doing – then all you need to do is do it better!

You've also got to make sure that the vehicle that you choose suits your personality and you're not trying to make your round peg fit in a square hole. I remember a time when I was consulting to a real estate firm and I originally went in to train the staff in sales skills. I was having a conversation one day with the business owner (I'll call her Sarah) and I asked her why she was doing it. It turned out that she was running her business, and her staff and premises, because that was her perception of how business should look. She said to me, 'Well, a proper business has staff and a proper building, that's what a real business looks like!' My response was, 'Who told you that?'

In my mind a proper business is one that makes a profit – actually makes real money. And if it can make that money easily, so much the better!' We kept talking and the truth was she didn't like working with people and didn't like the responsibility of the staff and the premises. None of the staff were really excited about working there either. On her own she was a dynamite saleswoman, but she was bogged down by a vehicle that didn't fit her. So we got rid of the building and we got rid of the staff and now she's really happy and she's making a lot of money. She fell into the trap of trying to fit into the conventional idea of what a 'real' business is. But a business is an entity that makes money. That's it! If you don't have that vehicle then you either need to leave and get another one, or re-tweak the one that you're already in so it gives you a fighting chance.

GET COMPLETELY FREE

'Create a Stampede of New Business and Profits'

The 10 rules of the successful entrepreneur. A powerful 10 day course on discovering the tools to turn yourself into a highly successful entrepreneur.

Go now to www.RichesFromBusiness.com/FreeGift

The Four Ways to Get Money

There are only four ways to make money.

1. Marry it or win it!

The first way is to win money or marry it. But let's face it, the chances of winning money are slim and your chance of marrying money is probably even slimmer. Plus you don't really have any control over either option. And even if you do turn out to be the one in a million to achieve wealth this way, what happens when it's gone? If you win the lottery, you might fritter it all away and wake up broke one day. There was a recent news story in the UK where a lottery winner was applying for a council house after blowing his entire £10 million winnings and managing to rack up huge debts as well! He might just be an idiot. But he's not alone – the statistics of lottery winners staying wealthy are dismal.

If you married money and it ran out (either the money or the spouse!), you've no way of regaining that wealth under your own steam. Winning the lottery or marrying into money isn't that likely in the first place so repeating it is particularly unrealistic.

2. Be an employee

The second way to make money is by having a job. Most people make money this way but very few become wealthy. In all the time I've been working I've only ever met one person who became financially independent at a young age by having a job. He was a single guy, never married, no kids. He was a foreigner for a corporate crew in an Asian country for about 18 to 20 years and he stashed everything away and invested in real estate. The taxes were very low and he became financially independent. But he's the only person I've ever met who has done it by working for someone else.

Of course, there are CEOs and senior executives of very large organisations that are making millions a year but they are certainly not working two days a week! I have met some of these people and a lot of them are workaholics. Their whole life is work, work, work and many of them cannot get off the treadmill because they need to keep up the image with a bigger house, car, boat.

Making money as an employee has very little advantages for you in the long term. We have all had it drummed into us that we should go to school, get a good education and a good job and if we do we'll be set up for life. And while that may have been true 50 years ago, it's not anymore. There is no such thing as a job for life. The average adult is expected to have several career changes during his or her lifetime. The only person getting rich from your long hours and hard work is the owner of the business. There are those that prefer this option because they don't want the responsibility of staff and premises, they think that a job will give them security, but a quick glance of the national newspaper will remind them that having a job is no longer as secure as it used to be. Job cuts are a constant spectre in modern business – especially public limited companies where shareholders' interests dominate.

I believe it's all a myth. You never have real security when you work for someone else. You never have control over the rest of the business and so while you may be doing a great job, others may not, and that incompetence leaves the business, and you, vulnerable. You pay your taxes on your income before the money you've earned even reaches your pocket. And the possibilities for tax advantages are limited. The opposite is true if you own a business. As an employee you're vulnerable to internal politics and strategy changes and unless you get on well with everyone, your name will always be close to the top of the list when things get tough. Is that really security?

3. Become an investor

The third way you can make money is by becoming an investor. Very often people confuse this with being in business, especially when it comes to property. Say you specialise in renovations and you buy old houses, renovate them, sell for a profit and move on to the next house. Some people would consider you a professional investor. You might even call yourself that. But you're not – you're in business. You are buying something, changing it and selling it – that sounds very much like a business to me. I know someone who makes serious money building single homes. He has three different designs and he builds those over and over again. People call him an investor, but he's not. He's a property developer/builder.

People assume that the rich get rich by investing, but they get rich in business and then invest their wealth in real estate and other assets. But where does that money come from? Usually it's from a business – the business ALWAYS comes first.

Investing is certainly important, but it's only relevant once you have something to invest.

4. Be a business owner or entrepreneur

By far the best way to make money is by being a business owner or entrepreneur. You have much more control over the outcome and there is no ceiling because you are not swapping your time for money. As an employee you can only ever swap your time for money, so there is no leverage opportunity.

Statistically, the vast majority of people make their money in business and then invest that money to create the wealth they seek. Sure you can make an income and invest that money too, but considering most people are struggling to meet their monthly commitments and pay their credit card debt there usually isn't a huge amount of money left at the end of the month to invest with. Business, on the other hand, provides a limitless vehicle to create the money you need to invest in your future AND have fun right now.

All you need to do is get the vehicle that is right for your market and implement some tried and tested protocols to ensure your business capitalises on its intrinsic opportunities and doesn't tie you in knots.

One of the mistakes I see time and again is the enthusiastic and skilled technician who takes the plunge into business for themselves. This is a commendable and often brave choice and certainly being in business is the best way to make money. But only if you set it up correctly and know your strengths and weaknesses. Just because you're a good joiner or an outstanding chef doesn't automatically make you a good business owner.

The skills you need to run a good business will probably not be the ones that prompted the decision in the first place. When you start a business you suddenly need to be a good salesperson too, a manager of people, an administrator and a planner. It isn't long before you never see the inside of the joinery shop, instead you're fighting fires and doing all the stuff you're neither trained for, nor good at, trying to juggle this monster you've created called your own business!

But it doesn't have to be that way. By taking the time to

make sure you have the right vehicle, your business really can create the lifestyle and money you dreamed of.

The key to making more money in a business

The key to making money in business is to understand the genuine purpose of business. It doesn't matter if you are a joiner or a chef or a construction magnate – you are in the business of making money. How you do that is the only thing that differs from business to business. You must serve your customers and add value, otherwise you won't be very good at your business and won't make money. You would have heard all this before, right? Well that is only half the truth. I am going to let you in on a secret. It's the secret of how the countless multi-millionaires I have met have really made their money in business. I am going to warn you, you may not like the secret, however, it is the truth. What I am about to tell you is not 'popular', or the knowledge via some academic who has never been in the real world. It is my experience and the experience of dozens and dozens of successful people who I actually know and many who I have made into millionaires. Here it is. The purpose of a business is to serve you first – and to make you money.

I know that most of the time we hear that business is about serving the customer and developing a reputation for quality and service. And certainly those things are important, but let's get real … If you are considering starting your own business – or have already done so – are you seriously trying to tell me that your decision was based on 'wanting to serve the customer?' That may be what you told other people, but it was also driven by your desire for a better life, more time, more control, more money! And there is absolutely nothing wrong with that. We've been brainwashed into believing that wanting more money is a bad thing – that it somehow makes us dishonourable. Nothing could be further from the truth.

If your business is doing well and you are making money, then by definition you are serving the customer. You are quite obviously delivering something to market that is wanted, needed and appreciated so you are doing a good thing – not fleecing people. It may be possible to fool people into buying a bad product once, but not twice! So the idea of business being a ruthless exploiter of vulnerability is really very outdated and just plain wrong.

This economy, and any other economy you can mention, was started by self-serving entrepreneurs who were very clear about the fact that they wanted to make a lot of money. In order to do that, they had to found businesses that delivered products and services that other people wanted.

Occasionally I have asked groups of people, 'What business are you in?' People reply that they are in, for example, the retail business or the business of being a mechanic. Never forget that, first and foremost, you are in the money business. If you remember that at all times you will automatically create phenomenal products. Because you know that the quickest way to make more money is by creating a product or service that other people want, and more importantly, knowing how to market it (we will get to that later). This is what separates the rich from the rest. They don't sit around wondering how to add value; they work out how to make more money.

I think that's actually why the rich have sometimes got bad press. Because others look at them and feel that all they are interested in is money. But that's the paradox. A successful business owner will stay focused on making more money knowing that the ONLY way to do that is to make better products, provide better service and surprise and delight their customers. They intrinsically know that the only way to make more money is to be better than their competitors. That's not ruthless – it's common sense.

Compare that to the person spending $20 a week on lottery tickets. That person isn't prepared to do anything for that money except buy a ticket. They aren't swapping their ideas, energy or dedication for that money. All they want is the money. That sounds much more ruthless to me. Statistically those people that do end up winning the lottery end up worse off than before they won it because they didn't exchange anything for it. They have no appreciation for the effort that it took to acquire it and no understanding of how to keep it.

I hang out with a lot of multi-millionaires and they all focus on the money. They're looking at it all the time. Now some rich people may say (in the desire to be politically correct), "Oh, money is just a way of keeping score." Rubbish! Just ask them if they are willing to keep score with pretend money instead of real money.

The 2004 Ig Nobel Prize for Psychology, for achievements that "make you laugh, then think" went to Daniel Simons of the University of Illinois and Christopher Chabris of Harvard. They asked a group of people to watch a video of a game of basketball. They were asked to count the number of passes that one of the sides made. During the video a woman in a gorilla suit walked onto the court for a full seven seconds, wandering among the players. At one point the gorilla even turned to the camera and beat her chest! Less than half the viewers saw the gorilla! Why? Because the viewers were so focused on counting the passes that they didn't see anything else, including a gorilla!

It's the same thing with the rich. They are rich because they focus on money. It's not a happy by-product of their business; it's the primary target. However, there is something else you need to know. If the only thing you care about is making money, then you won't make much either. I will give you an example. Have you ever tried to buy a used car from a salesperson that only wanted your money? You probably didn't buy the car did you? You have to make money a target, but you also have to focus on something else as well. I will tell you about that soon when we get to the all-important 'success drivers'.

It's the same with anything – you get what you focus on. In a relationship, if you don't spend any time together and don't focus on each other, the relationship will fall apart. It's really not that complicated – if two people don't have fun together, don't communicate or laugh together then how are they ever going to stay together? And what happens when that focus goes outside the relationship – affairs happen. It's just because their attention and focus have shifted.

If you don't focus on something it doesn't happen or it disappears. If you don't focus on your kids then one day they'll be gone and you'll realise you don't know them. If you don't focus on your health you'll pay the price of being ill. If you don't take care of your body and treat it well, it will deteriorate.

It's the same in business! If you focus on adding value then you'll add value, whether it is financially viable or not. If you focus on having the best customer service then you'll keep your customers very happy, even the ones who never pay on time or are more trouble than they are worth. If you focus on money then you'll make money. Make it a priority.

I remember Daniel really well. He came to one of my seminars and, boy, was he struggling! He worked really long hours and came home every night feeling like he had been whipped. He felt like there was no way out. Daniel realised over the course of the weekend that his goal was to be in business. He also realised that is exactly why he wasn't making money – because he wasn't in 'the money business' or the business of making money. When he shifted his focus, everything changed, and he began to make money. He adopted many of the Financial Acceleration $uccess Techniques (FA$T) detailed in the second half of this book and now he's doing really well.

How to Revolutionise Your Income: The Power of Understanding Your 'Success Drivers'

Now in case you are starting to think, 'Gee, this Brendan Nichols guy is just into the money', let me repeat something important in case you have missed it. Money is ONLY good for two things: 'Get a life, give a life.' It is to create a life for yourself and to create a life for others. It is to provide FREEDOM for you and your loved ones and for giving away to some great charities. That is its only purpose. If you are trying to create an image for yourself and impress others then I think you are missing a big point. At the end of your life the only thing you take with you is the person you have become. The money stays here, so you might as well enjoy it while you are around and become a person you and the people you care about can be proud of.

As someone who teaches others how to make more money

from their business, one of the things that causes business owners the biggest problem is the idea that they are in business to make money. Trust me, I've heard all the reasons on earth for why people are in business – everything from the predictable 'adding value' and 'to serve the customer' to the more original, although no less realistic, 'to change the world'.

Just so you're REALLY clear on this … Repeat after me:

I'm in business to make money!

Whether you achieve that or not depends on your success drivers.

Here is the full list of all 12 success drivers.

1.   Recognition

2.   Fame

3.   Achievement

4.   Praise

5.   Money

6.   Satisfaction of a job well done

7.   The pursuit of excellence

8.   Competition

9.   Empire builders
        (wanting to create a business empire, eg, Richard
        Branson)

10.   Contribution to humanity
        (philanthropist)

11.   Productivity/busyness
        (hard working people who love to be busy and
        accomplish lots of things)

12.   Creativity

Take at look at these 12 psychological success drivers. I want you to go through the list and rank them in order of importance. Let's say you looked at the list and decided that number 6 – satisfaction of a job well done – was your primary motivator at work. Write '1' next to number 6. Maybe you're very competitive and are driven to be the best in everything you do, then number 8 is probably your number 1 driver. Work down the list and allocate a rank to each driver.

By the way, I'm not asking you what you want your drivers to be, or what you hope they are and what you think your partner hopes they are or what they might be in the future, I'm talking about right now. Be honest – what is it about your work or your business that is really driving you?

I run this exercise in my seminars on wealth creation in business and I've literally had people cry once they found this out! I vividly remember Lance – he was a CEO of a big company, he had two secretaries, a monster-sized office, a big salary – and apart from owning his own home – he had nothing but a small super fund. He was around 50 years of age and had worked all his life. He was sitting there after doing this exercise and he looked like a bomb had gone off next to him. He was stunned. He actually came up to me during the break and said, 'That was one of the most profound things I have ever done in my life. Now I know why I am successful but not wealthy! The thing that I care about most is recognition and the pursuit of excellence. All my life I have worked towards that, and funnily enough, that is exactly what I've got. However, I spent most of money on all the right toys because they got me recognition. And I never went into business for myself because I wanted recognition from the owners of the company.'

Just understanding what was really driving him was a relief. He'd worked hard and was genuinely good at his job. He had always been confused as to why he couldn't translate that obvious ability into wealth. Now he knew, and because he knew, he was able to change his life.

Take a look at your list – I'm about to do something really amazing. I'm going to predict something that's going to blow you away. If you are currently not making as much money as you'd like, and let's face it, you wouldn't be reading this book if you were – then I'm going to dazzle you with my predictive powers ... Drum roll please ... Money doesn't figure in your top two.

What I've found over and over again when I run this

exercise in seminars is that those people who make the money in business are the ones who have money usually in the first two of their priorities. It could be, for example, that money is number 2 and number 1 is competition (or the other way around – money may be number 1). Money is very often a by-product of what they do in order to meet their other higher-ranking drivers.

These success drivers are psychological aspects of our nature. They represent what we really value. Very often people are completely unaware of them.

I will let you in on a secret. When I first started in business, my two drivers were recognition and satisfaction of a job well done. No wonder I didn't make any money! Because I was about to disappear down a financial abyss, I automatically made money a priority. I had to – it was sink or swim.

These days my two key motivators are very different. Money and contribution to humanity are at the top of the list. As far as contribution to humanity goes that is very specific. Sure, I donate money to charities, however, that is not where I believe my biggest contribution is. My stated purpose for my clients is, 'I take business people and put cash in their pocket.' I am extremely clear and focused on that goal. You have no idea how happy it makes me when I help people get out of the rat race and leave their life of stress and chaos behind – for good!

When I first met Ross Mclean he was encountering some challenges and felt he was not achieving anywhere near his potential. Ross wrote to me recently and said, 'Your powerful strategies have massively increased my success. It's put so much money in my bank account that money has become a non-issue – I am now financially free! My lifestyle is now truly amazing and I am living the life of my dreams. Brendan, your information is awesome!' To me that is better than winning the lottery – to hear that news just makes me feel so good because I know that what I'm doing is really making a difference to people. And that meets my primary driver.

So you have to first understand what it is that is unconsciously driving you, so that you can tap into that power rather than rail against it. At the same time, if money is important to you then it has to be a focus – and if it's not an unconscious natural focus then it needs to become one! Just like the students who didn't see the gorilla in the Harvard experiment, you won't see opportunities to make money if you don't make it a priority.

Take Susan, for example: she came to a lot of my seminars and was one of the hardest-working people I have ever met. She loved achieving goals and being incredibly busy and she easily did the work of two people. But she found it really hard to make money from her business. When she prioritised her drivers she realised that productivity/busyness was number 1 and recognition was number 2. Money was nowhere in sight.

This is such a toxic perspective. Somewhere in our evolution we have been led to believe that busy is good. Everything in modern society is set up for speed and efficiency and if you don't have at least five programs open on your computer at any one time then you're a slacker! But just because you are busy, does not mean you will make money. You have to be busy at the tasks that produce money. Everything else is just fluff and bluster!

Tony also attended one of my seminars on making more money in business. His priorities were creativity and productivity – in that order. Again money was nowhere to be seen. Surprise, surprise, he was incredibly creative and his workload was amazing but he consistently found it hard to make money from his efforts.

John W Gardner once said, 'All of us celebrate our values in our behaviour.' I would take that a step further and say, 'All of us celebrate our values in our results!'

Now all this may sound a little contradictory. On one hand, I'm saying your business has one purpose and one purpose only – to make money. On the other hand, I'm saying that if money is your only focus you'll probably not reach that target. But you need to separate the idea of your business – your vehicle – from you the person. You the person may want recognition, you might be driven to be the best. That's great, because if you incorporate those success drivers into your business then the vehicle can't help but make money … if money is also up at the top of the list.

If money is number 1 and money is all you want then you won't know what to do – you won't be psychologically influenced toward a particular strategy. That is the problem with people who just want to win the lottery. All they want is money. However, to make money, money needs to be high on the list – plus some additional success drivers! If money's important but you're more interested in pursuing excellence and building an empire then you will probably end up with all three!

Let's take Cathy as an example because a lot of people can relate to her. She has a job and is very good at it. She's diligent and hard working, is of above-average intelligence and committed to being successful. She has been to several wealth creation seminars, in particular, real estate investment seminars, all of which provided information that could have transformed her fortunes. Yet she still makes less than $50K a year and only has one real estate investment, which isn't performing very well. The bottom line is she THINKS she wants more money and really wants to be more successful. So much so that she's started to feel desperate and buys lottery tickets in the hope she might pull off the big one. If you asked her, she would say money is high on the list. And on the surface that would seem to be the case.

However, the truth is very different. On the psychological success drivers, praise scored number 1, satisfaction of a job well done was number 2 and number 3 was competition. What was really driving her was she wanted to be the most successful person in her company so the boss would praise her for a job well done. To her shock, money was not even in her top 5. Interestingly enough, Cathy met every one of her top three drivers.

At the other end of the spectrum is a very angry young man I recently met. Let's call him Robert. Robert doesn't want to help anyone, he just wants to make a lot of money so he does not have to work. He doesn't want success or to improve himself or to work for the money or take a risk, he just wants the money. He has a history of trouble and wants to win the lottery. Money is all he covets. Needless to say, he has none. You can't make money long term unless you have another driver. It's a bit like what Zig Ziglar said: 'I can get whatever I want as long as I help other people get what they want.' Frank Bettger, a master salesman who wrote the 1947 sales classic How I Raised Myself From Failure to Success in Sales says something very similar, 'The quickest way to get what you want is to find out what other people want and help them get it.'

You need to work out what drives you, NOT what you think drives you or what you wish drove you. And the best way to do that is to look at your results. Look at the list and see what you are actually experiencing just now. Chances are that will hold a clue to what you are driven by.

By consciously adding money to that mix you can still meet your unconscious drivers but if you also focus on money you will be able to reap the rewards. If making lots of money from your business is not part of that focus, you won't make lots of money from your business.

Take me, for example. As I've said, my number 1 and 2 (or joint first!) is money and contribution to humanity. I therefore work through those aspects to achieve my financial success. I now operate a business that practises what I preach and I've been able to help thousands of other business owners do the same. I get a buzz from doing my seminars and for being described by my entrepreneur clients as 'the guy that puts cash profits in my pocket'. I really love it when happy business owners refer me on to others because they are so excited about what I've helped them do in their business. It reminds me of my contribution and I love that. My business also allows me to honour my other driver – by donating significant amounts of money to causes that I'm really passionate about. So the business also allows me to feed my psychological need for contribution in terms of philanthropy. And it also allows me to have a great life and go on some amazing adventures.

Say a wealthy individual came along and was full of praise for me and what I do. So much so, that he made me an offer to go and work for him in a business I found morally questionable but he would pay me 10 million dollars to do it. If I didn't know my own success drivers and was only focused on making money then I might seriously consider that offer. But because I do, because I'm not actually that bothered about receiving praise from others and am far more motivated to know that I've done a good job, I wouldn't accept the offer. Because I know that this new position would give me no opportunity to support my causes – and maybe even be part of the problem – I wouldn't accept the offer. I wouldn't be able to make a contribution in the way I value and so no money would be enough in order for me to accept that offer.

I could rev you up and tell you that you're going to get rich, but seriously, unless you make money a priority in your life you won't. You may be reading this and realise that money doesn't actually figure in your top three and feel despondent. You may realise that you have an employee mentality and are wondering whether you can consciously change it.

The good news is, yes, you can.

The minute you truly want something, your value system will change. Remember we talked about the snap point in Chapter 2. The snap point is the point that you reach when things are really bad. Whatever value system you have been running clearly doesn't work and you're getting yourself into deeper and deeper trouble. You crash and burn – and in that moment you change. Something inside you changes, what you value, what you want, what you're prepared to do, what you're not prepared to do – it all changes in an instant and a new future emerges. When I started my very first company I really doubt if money would have been in my top five. It was probably way down at the bottom. Looking back, I took the opportunity because the previous owner was blowing my trumpet and saying how good I'd be at it. It was ego – a looking-good, going-nowhere moment! It was ludicrous. I had no business plan, and more importantly, did not know the specific formula that I now teach that makes real money in a business. I had no experience whatsoever and I set off to pull off mission impossible. It was only when the business was failing miserably and the kudos of 'having my own real estate business' wore off and the reality of not having any money to support my family arrived with a thump, that everything changed. Money wasn't in my top three, and unsurprisingly, I didn't make any. But when I sat at that beat-up formica table with my head in my hands you better believe that money moved up that list really fast.

Let's just take a minute to explore this a little more, because it's important. The reason reaching a snap point is so often the catalyst for change is because of emotion. Most people don't wake up one sunny day and decide to change things.

Usually their life is pretty bad – things go from bad to worse until the emotional pain is so great that they literally snap! That may be real pain, like mine, where I really was in deep financial trouble, or it could be imagined pain, in terms of: if I don't make this work then my family are going to suffer. One of the wonderful things about human nature is that we will invariably do more for someone we love than we will ever do for ourselves. I am confident that had I not had a wife and young daughter depending on me I would have been stuck in that mess for a lot longer.

I didn't realise it at the time but the emotional pain I was in as I sat in my scruffy kitchen was enough to shake things up and my success drivers changed in an instant.

And yours can too.

GET COMPLETELY FREE

'3 Reasons People Sabotage Their Success (that very few people know about) and How to Change It'

Your mindset is vital to your success. These Powerful Secrets show you why people destroy their success. Don't fall victim to being blind-sided by a Mack truck. This mini e-book will show you how to bypass these hidden mine fields and program yourself for success. **Value $47.00**

Go now to www.RichesFromBusiness.com/FreeGift

The Four Levels of Wealth Mastery

There are four levels to mastering wealth. Very few people ever move to levels 3 and 4. And yet this is definitely where you want to be. Let's take a good look at the levels and see how you can increase your mastery of money.

Level 1:
The condition of struggle

The condition of struggle is the most painful level of them all. It's no fun! Struggle – as the name would suggest – is the level where you feel you can never make enough money. Some people struggle because they don't have the skills or motivation to make money, but by far the majority of the Struggle Street population stays there because of something much more insidious. The number one reason that people are in struggle is because of their income ceiling. An income ceiling is the absolute most amount of money you are willing to accept.

At first you might think that sounds ridiculous, and that's why it is so insidious. This income ceiling acts as an unconscious barrier to your own success and you don't even know it's there!

When I met Emily, I have to confess she looked older that her 27 years. I sat across the table from her and the first thing I noticed was that she looked tired. Her brown hair hung close to her skin and her eyes lacked sparkle. She wasn't depressed, but she sure wasn't excited. She began to tell me about her situation and what had been plaguing her for several years.

'Everyone tells me that I have enormous talent, at work it's common knowledge that I do the work of two people, yet I can never seem to get ahead. I just can't seem to make enough money, I have even started a second job at night, just to try and make some extra cash.' The end of her sentence trailed off in despair.

I asked her, 'What kind of work do you do Emily?' She told me, 'I work as a receptionist by day and a waitress by night. Five days a week in my receptionist job and seven nights as a waitress.'

I was shocked – that's a lot of hours. So I suggested, 'Have you tried to get other work?' She told me that she had worked in other jobs but that they all made about the same amount of money.

Of course, I asked how much that was. Emily told me that she made about $14 an hour. And we both agreed it wasn't much money.

I switched track. Looking directly at Emily, I asked the question that changed everything. 'Emily, how much do you think you are worth?'

Emily looked puzzled, 'Well, I know I would like a lot more than $14 an hour, that's for sure!'

'Yes, I understand that, but what I want to know is what you think you are worth. You see, everyone has an income ceiling. Your income ceiling is the amount of money you are willing to accept. For example, I know people who would like to make $200 an hour but the reality is they make $20 an hour. Some of them switch businesses or get a different job but they always seem to make the same amount of money.'

After a fairly long silence, in which it was obvious that Emily was giving the matter serious consideration, she looked up at me and said, 'Okay, if I was to be completely honest I would have to say that even though I would like to make more money, the truth is that I feel that $14 an hour is about what I am willing to accept. Gee, I don't like to admit that, but unfortunately it feels like the truth.'

Let me elaborate on this, just so you can get more of an understanding of the income ceiling. If we can understand it, then we have the ability to get out of it. The problem with the income ceiling is that it's a bit like the fish in the water. Mr Fish probably has no idea he's in water. He just accepts that is his normal environment. But because we have a greater understanding than the fish, we know the fish is in water because we are looking from the outside in.

If you want to change things, you have to get out of the

water and look from the outside in. Looking into your life to see what results you're achieving will tell you a great deal about what you think is possible. Someone who has an income ceiling is usually looking from the inside out. They can't see their problem because they are inside it; they have to get outside before they can see it. It is a bit like when you have been trying to figure out a complex problem and you decide to change your surroundings and say, go for a walk on the beach, or you start talking about it with a friend. Just having to explain the situation to someone else gives you another perspective – and suddenly the answer appears.

Everyone has an income ceiling. I know sales trainers who work with some of the top-selling salespeople in the country. Often they are making a quarter of a million dollars a year. Each year during training they may decide to set the next year's goal at $350,000. Every year it's the same result – the high earners will make their quarter of a million dollars in the first three-quarters of the year, but sometime around October their momentum stops and they just can't seem to make much more. No one could understand why – not even the salespeople themselves. There was plenty of time to reach the target and certainly no lack of ability to meet the new goal, but they were being unconsciously trapped by their income ceiling.

In their mind, $250,000 was the top of what they legitimately believed they could ask for. It was a mental milestone and they couldn't justify why they were worth more than that. Now don't get me wrong, $250,000 a year is pretty damn good, but this happens to people at $14 an hour too – it has nothing to do with the money and everything to do with attitude and self-perception.

Our income ceiling is the amount of money we are willing to accept. It is the subconscious limit to your earning capacity and it is this that limits your earning potential more than anything else.

There's a great poem in Napoleon Hill's classic book Think and Grow Rich that is worth sharing here ...

I bargained with Life for a penny,
And Life would pay no more,
However I begged at evening
When I counted my scanty store.

For Life is a just employer,
He gives you what you ask,
But once you have set the wages,
Why, you must bear the task.

I worked for a menial's hire,
Only to learn, dismayed,
That any wage I had asked of Life,
Life would have willingly paid.

Some external unjust force is not keeping you from wealth – very often your own mind is doing a remarkably good job all on its own! Like so many people, Emily bargained with life for a penny. She didn't believe she was worth any more than that. Once we'd finished talking she looked like a shroud had been lifted from her.

Imagine that you took a very poor person from a ghetto and put them in the penthouse suite of a 5-star hotel. How many nights do you think they would be able to stay there before they started to feel uncomfortable? The truth is that very few people could stay there. After a while their discomfort would make them go back to the familiarity of the ghetto. Our income ceiling is a lot like that, and this accounts for why so many people who win the lottery are back where they started within five years.

To get an indication of what your income ceiling is, you have to imagine going for a job you really want and being told what it will pay. Or imagine writing up an invoice for a client and imagine you charged $14 an hour. Keep raising the hourly rate or imagine being offered more money until you reach a point that is uncomfortable. You really have to engage with this process and imagine yourself in that situation. It's not an exact science but a friend of mine told me a great story of how she found out her income ceiling.

She and some friends were having dinner one night and one of them was telling the group about how he had got a contract position with a very large prestigious international organisation. Everyone was very excited about the news and they started talking about the role and inevitably the topic of pay came up. He wasn't sure what to charge and so they discussed it. He decided to ask for $1000 an hour. Everyone laughed but he was serious. My friend said, 'I was impressed but the idea of actually asking for that amount was unthinkable for me. And strangely, a part of me found it almost offensive ... I knew I'd hit some sort of internal barrier.' She had hit some internal barrier – she'd met her income ceiling up close and personal. Oh, by the way, her friend asked for $1000 an hour – and got it!

Don't bargain with life for a penny.

It is this low expectation that lies at the heart of an employee system. Business owners know that most people totally underestimate what they are worth. They have a ceiling that means that they only expect little pay increases each year. Anything more than that makes them nervous. Working out for yourself what your income ceiling is can be very enlightening. A good place to start is what you make right now. Try adding a few digits to the figure and see how uncomfortable it starts to make you feel.

You have to demand more from life and yourself – when you do, it will deliver.

There is a postscript to this story. At the time of writing, Emily was in deep discussion with a multi-millionaire about forming a partnership in her own business. She reached a point where she had had enough of her situation and decided to do something about it.

Level 2:
The condition of success

Level 2 of wealth mastery is called the condition of success. Success for most people is a condition that looks good to those around them. A friend of mine is considered to be very successful. He is a partner in a high-profile law firm, works very long hours, drives an expensive European car, has a big house and he knows the 'right people'. By most people's standards he is a 'success'. Everyone thinks he has lots of money but the reality is that all that money goes into looking good. Like I said, 'looking-good, going-nowhere!' And in most of these cases this is literally true – they get a few weeks of holidays a year, work like dogs and get to go nowhere!

Yet in private conversations he has revealed to me that he hates his work and just wants to get out – but he doesn't think he can because he would lose everything. The reality is less dramatic and he may lose the kudos and high opinion others have of him. He would no longer get to play the part of 'wealthy successful lawyer'. Contrast this to another friend of mine who drives an ordinary car and couldn't care less what others think of him. His neighbours and casual acquaintances do not regard him as a successful person because he does not have the 'trappings of success'. However, what they don't know is that he has over 8 million dollars in net assets.

In your quest for success, make sure the trappings of success do not become exactly that – trappings. Who are the trappings for – yourself or other people? Am I saying that you have to have money and not enjoy the finer things of life? Not at all! What I am saying is that if you stop at level 2 then you are only half way up the mountain. The condition of success can be a very dangerous point on the journey.

Take David, for example. He was a very successful

businessperson who came to me for a consultation. When David walked into the room he looked like someone who had just drunk six cups of coffee laced with three parts of adrenalin. He sat down and quickly cut to the chase, 'I own three very successful businesses but one of them doesn't make a profit, in fact it's actually costing me money.'

Raising my eyebrows, I said, 'Sounds to me like you have two successful businesses!'

At which point he became a little defensive. 'No, not at all – even though I have to use the profits of the other two businesses to prop it up, it's a success because that business employs over 40 people, while the other two businesses employ just a few people.'

I could already see the problem. 'Let me ask you a question David, what are your real reasons for wanting to keep this business?'

It took several minutes to get to the truth. There was always another excuse put forward about why it was a valid business but eventually David admitted that his real reason for keeping the business was that people in his local community looked up to him and perceived him to be a very successful person because he had a big office with 40 people who worked for him. David was stuck in the 'success condition'. Or as I like to call it, looking-good, going-nowhere!

Or what about John? When he first started attending my seminars he was already making a lot of money. Using the principles I outlined, his income skyrocketed. However, there was one big problem. As his income rose, so did his spending. John had to have every new toy on the market. He had all the latest bikes and would buy new cars like most people buy a new outfit. He would drive the latest model Porsche, get bored with it and then go out and buy the latest BMW. Life was fun and exciting but he wasn't really capitalising on his wealth. In many ways, he wasn't very different from David. He still wasn't fulfilled, despite the money. Both David and John were more concerned about image rather than being clever about their money or their time. John had achieved success in many ways – and he did have the cash to be frivolous. But there was no strategy, no big picture so that he could continue to enjoy that lifestyle – it was all about excess and immediate gratification. And there was no real joy. He got bored faster than a goldfish. He had a great time getting it out of his system, but it wasn't his long-term objective, because there was no framework in place to ensure that this newfound wealth stayed in place!

Why do people get stuck in the 'success condition'?

The reason people get stuck in the success condition almost always relates to seeking recognition. We all crave some form of recognition and want to feel valued and significant. However, this element of human nature can become pronounced when a person doesn't feel okay about who they are. It can be a symptom of low self-esteem. Often those driven hard by a need to show off and to be recognised are trying to mask their own insecurities. On some level they actually feel inadequate and are driven to prove there is nothing wrong with them!

In other words, people start to desire recognition because they believe deep down that they are insignificant.

Wanting to stand out and be significant is a normal part of human psychology. It becomes a problem when it is the dominating force of that personality. Very often, as is the case with those stuck in the success condition, it becomes their jailer. It is normal to want to prove yourself when you haven't been successful before, however, it's not normal if you spend most of your life proving to yourself and others that you are worthy of their attention and admiration. You are okay whether you are successful or not. The reality is that if someone is in the success condition, it cost them time and money. It's just like David in the story above. His time and money were being used to prove to others that he was okay. If people want to do that, that's fine by me, however, there are a lot more exciting and satisfying ways to live.

Level 3:
The condition of affluence

To me this is the Holy Grail. Level 3 is the condition of affluence and it is exactly what this book as all about – finding a business vehicle that makes you rich AND creates a phenomenal life.

The only reason you really want money is to create some kind of emotion. For some people that may be a feeling of power, authority or security. There is no right answer, and no right emotion, but knowing what it might be is really important, because money alone will probably not give you that emotion. The emotion comes from how you create the money and who you become.

A lot of people aspire to a level of wealth that means they can retire. I've tried that, actually I've retired a few times, but it just doesn't work for me. After I've sat on beaches for five months, I'm done with sitting on a beach. Sure sitting on a beach for five months is better than working in a job you hate. But sitting on a beach to recharge your batteries, or skiing three times a year and then returning to a business you love – that's just so much fun.

The condition of affluence is about having a business that you enjoy, that makes you more money than you'll ever probably need and having the freedom to enjoy the spoils of your work. Think of it more as semi-retirement!

Affluence is an opportunity to explore all the other wonderful things the world has to offer – to go back to school and study something completely new, or to learn how to pilot a plane – essentially, having a business that allows you to have the best of both worlds. I really enjoy what I do and I miss it if I'm away for too long but it's an amazing feeling to know I can go for months at a time and still make money even while I'm not there.

Getting people to move from level 1 to 2 and then onto 3 is one of the greatest thrills of my life. Whether it's through the seminars I teach or the audio programs I produce or whether clients are part of my inner circle coaching program, the results speak for themselves and I'm able to meet my psychological drive for contribution and make serious money. AND so are my clients. It's a perfect synergy and win/win for everyone involved. If you want more information on how you can have this kind of life then go to www.RichesFromBusiness.com where you can learn more.

Level 4:
The condition of wealth

John is a friend of mine. About a year ago he sold his business for millions of dollars and invested the lot. I remember seeing him just after he closed the deal. He was ecstatic, 'Brendan, I never have to work again, it's fantastic!'

John had certainly moved into the condition of wealth.

But it would be remiss of me to leave the story there. It may be true that the condition of wealth is the pinnacle of success in terms of wealth creation. When you are in this position you don't have to work another day in your life. You are completely financially independent and free.

But it's not all it's cracked up to be … eight months after retiring John was bored stiff and has now found another venture. The funny thing was that John already had level 3 success and a great life before he sold his business. It made a ton of money; he spent a couple of months a year on holiday or away from the business and when he was working it was only for a couple of days a week, on average.

People dream of reaching the condition of wealth but they fail to realise that working gives them rewards way beyond just money. Just ask someone who has recently retired! They often become bored and lose interest in life. Their social network is removed and they don't get to feel part of something, they don't enjoy the camaraderie of working life and don't get to feel as though their contribution matters. These are important needs that are met at work – even if you don't really enjoy it sometimes!

While I think it is great that you work toward the condition of wealth, finding a happy medium at level 3 is, in my opinion, your ultimate goal. We all still need to meet our psychological drivers. Lying around on a beach doesn't give you an opportunity to make a contribution or pursue excellence, does it?

CHAPTER 9

The Foundation of Building Wealth

Good debt versus bad debt

I'll warn you up front – you're not going to like this chapter. Over the last 10 or 20 years the media has systematically fed us stories of wealth and prosperity. The property boom has meant that many people have become wealthy – or at least they appear to be – although it's often not real net wealth. For example, a friend of mine who is stuck in level 2 – the condition of success – now has a house that is worth several million dollars. On paper he is a multi-millionaire, but he can't sell his house. If he sells and downsizes, he makes money but then he won't be recognised by his peers as a success, so he is upsizing and going into more debt! The house he was in was already way too big for him, so what's the point?

Sure, people have made a lot of money out of property but some are carrying an enormous amount of debt or they are cash flow poor – they simply do not have the cash coming in every month to go out and have that amazing life right NOW. There is a saying in real estate, 'you make your money when you buy', which means if you buy well you make money, but in reality the only time you make money is when you sell. I know people who have 30 or more properties, which sounds really impressive but the reality is that many of these people don't own all those properties – their bank does. They have a tiny percentage of equity in all the properties and the rest is borrowed money.

Looking at debt worldwide, it's scary. Let's start in the United States because whatever happens there will eventually be felt around the world. For years banks were lending happily to people to buy their house. This kicked off a property boom and soon everyone was buying houses, even people who really couldn't afford one! These people were classed as 'sub prime' – as the name suggests they were not prime candidates for loans. The banks didn't really mind because it was a very lucrative market, and besides, the underlying property asset was increasing in value and so that would compensate for the added risk.

The banks didn't actually want to keep the debt so they packaged up the mortgages and sold them on the financial markets to companies like superannuation funds etc. The bank would lend the money, at say 6%, and then on-sell the debt by offering investment vehicles, at say 5%. That way the bank could recoup the cash and continue to lend again and again to the mortgage market while removing the risk and skimming off the profit on the top. Happy days!

Well, at least until the property market slowed down. More

and more people defaulted on their loans. The underlying asset was then not worth the mortgage and everyone was in trouble. Because the mortgages were actually sold-on it was like adding lots of little bits of rotten apple to a jam in the hope that the good apples would mask the taste. Only now there is so much rotten apple, the jam is off. That's what the sub prime problem means. And the real problem is that the world financial institutions don't actually know how bad the problem is and that is making everyone VERY nervous. Banks all around the world are being forced to write-off billions in bad debt and the credit crunch is now a global reality.

Property booms are all very well but the debt you have to carry to pull them off would make most people's eyes water. The only real money is realised money. It's money that you have actually made. You could try to sell a few properties but with credit controls being tightened there are less people in the market who are in a position to buy. You could hold on to them and hope it passes, but if your mortgage isn't fixed at a particular interest rate, you might be in for a bumpy ride.

The simple fact of the matter is that there is good debt and bad debt – but too much of any debt is a bad thing and I don't care what anyone says to the contrary!

The foundations of your wealth creation are very important – just like they are in a house. You wouldn't try to build a beautiful home on sand, for example. When an architect and builder build a house they spend most of the time getting 'out the ground' and making sure the foundations are right. If you visited the site everyday you wouldn't notice any real progress for months because this structural stuff isn't that exciting and it doesn't look like your home is actually getting anywhere. But get it wrong and your home will sink!

Wealth is exactly the same.

The concept of good debt and bad debt is very simple. Good debt is debt that makes you money and bad debt doesn't. But before you get too excited there isn't a lot of debt that makes you money! Personally, I don't like debt of any kind. I've only ever used debt to start up my first business and since then (touch wood), I've never had to do that again.

I do use debt to fund real estate purchases but that's all. I would never dream of buying anything else on credit. For example, I own my own car and it's a very nice car too, but I don't owe any money on it.

The idea of buying a new car on credit is stupid. Say you go into a dealership and buy an $80,000 car. You already know that the minute you drive it 15 metres up the road its value plummets to $65,000 because of depreciation. That's bad enough, so why would you get finance for that car when it means that you will end up paying about $130,000 to $160,000 for that car. It still depreciates at the same rate so all you've done is paid over the odds for a cash-guzzling liability!

If you want to buy a new car – buy it and enjoy it. But if you can't buy that car without debt then buy a car that you can afford without debt.

Sure, I understand that you have to look the part in business but you can do that without buying a brand new car.

And then there is my personal favourite – credit card debt. Don't get me wrong, I love credit cards. They are extremely convenient and if you use them correctly they can be a real bonus. I buy as much as I possibly can on credit card because I get points toward travel when I do, but when the bill comes in it's paid in full – immediately.

I can't put this any clearer for you – if you have credit card debt the ONLY person who will ever get rich is the credit card company. I'm not kidding – you have to handle this as your number one priority.

Don't buy anything that you can't afford. It's as simple and as unsexy as that. Credit card debt is financial suicide. There was a fuss a few years ago when the head of Barclay's Bank was involved in a United Kingdom government inquiry into the credit card industry. The head of credit cards even admitted that he does not use a Barclay Card because it's too expensive.

Just put that in perspective for a moment: how would you feel about one of the big cola companies if the global CEO came out and said, 'I never drink the stuff'? Would you wonder why not? Would it put you off the product? You bet it would, and yet when the head of a global credit business says virtually the same thing, most people didn't give it much thought. Yet he's a man who knows the real cost of credit – so when he says it's not a great idea then trust me, it's not a great idea!

Seriously, do you think the credit card companies offer you the opportunity to pay off a minimum balance each month because they are being nice? Do you think that they offer you an increased credit limit because they think you're a good person? Do you think it's just for your convenience that there are thousands of credit cards on offer at any one time – or is it because it's an incredibly lucrative business for the credit card companies'.

If you seriously want to create a wealth foundation, not just the illusion of one, then the first thing that you need to do is pay off all your bad debt. This is debt that isn't making you any money. That means that if you want to buy a new big screen colour TV, don't buy it until you've got the money to buy it. It doesn't make you any money.

The first step is to create what I call a debt annihilation payment plan. It might not be very enticing and it's certainly not very exciting but I'm deadly serious if you want to be wealthy as opposed to wealthy-looking and stressed about maintaining that illusion. If you want to go on a holiday, then you've got to figure out how you're going to make the extra money to go. Being lazy and getting a loan for the holiday is not the solution. If I put a gun to your head and said you need to figure out how to come up with say 5, 10, 20 thousand dollars to go on an overseas vacation and I'm going to pull the trigger if you don't figure it out, then you're going to figure it out. If you go into debt, you don't get to exercise your creativity and find solutions! Henry Ford said, 'Thinking is the hardest work there is, that's why no one engages in it.'

If you are seriously in debt then you may have to make some arrangements with your creditors. You need to get some good financial advice. Find someone that you can trust who could help you restructure your debt and make arrangements to pay it off as quickly as possible. And if that means selling that new car, then sell it. Get something smaller, downsize if you have to, in order to go back to your foundations and reinforce them. Think of it as though you were stripping back your home so you could strengthen your foundations for an even more beautiful home. Park your ego to one side and just do it!

Pay yourself first

This may seem contradictory to the idea of debt as, after all, it is because people want to pay themselves first or seek initial reward that so many get into so much trouble.

But this means something slightly different. This is about devoting a percentage of your net income to savings or investment. So as soon as you make any money you should pay yourself first. Don't buy anything, not even food, until you pay yourself first. You should be paying yourself between 10% or 20% of your earnings.

This idea has been around for a very long time and was originally connected to tithing – giving a percentage of your earnings to the church or some charitable cause. This is actually something that I do, but what I'm talking about is giving a percentage of your earnings to YOU before you pay for anything else.

But don't get too excited, this can only happen once you've cleared all your bad debt. So first of all you annihilate your debt and then you start paying yourself. You have to make this a habit. The satisfaction that you get in the beginning if you've never done this before is great. Having money, even a little, and seeing it grow creates a momentum that can take on a life of its own. You are able to look back over a year and see your savings account accumulate. And the best thing of all is you'll realise it wasn't that hard to make happen.

Part of getting money is getting money. That's not a misprint. What I mean is that part of the process of getting more money is just getting some money. You need to get into the habit of accumulating money. How much you then accumulate is entirely up to you but without the initial habit of accumulating anything, you won't make progress. Making money is more about your mindset than it is about your actions. Taking the time to habitually accumulate money, even if it's just a little in the beginning, influences your mental picture of money. You have to see yourself getting ahead and making real financial progress. That's why it's so important to eliminate debt to start with because it's impossible to get ahead when you have bad debt.

One of the stupidest things I have ever heard is people who have huge credit card debt but justify it saying, 'Yeah but I've got $5000 in my savings account.' Well then you're an idiot … You receive maybe 5% interest (if you're lucky) on your savings but are paying probably 12% or more on your credit card. That's crazy.

If you have to start small, then so be it. Again put your pride aside and do what needs to be done. You have to make small shifts to your psychology so that you can begin to believe that wealth creation is real and not just some fantasy future. If I put you in a 100 metre race and you came in dead last every time, what would that do to your psychology? How would you feel about yourself? How enthusiastic would you be about entering your next 100 metre race? But if in the next race you were second last, would your spirits rise? You would be motivated to keep going because you could see improvement. Well, money is exactly the same. So is anything else in life, if we can see improvement we are much more likely to remain motivated and reach our goal.

You don't need to go from zero to hero in five minutes, you just need to make some improvement early on so you can adapt your mindset to accommodate the possibility that it might work! If after a few months of paying yourself first you look at your bank statement and see it growing steadily, you've got no idea what that does for your psychology. So you've got to pay yourself first. And you've got to be ruthless.

Nothing gets taken out of that account. Nothing. Put it in a high yield account, preferably have it automatically deducted to that account every month. If possible, make sure there is no card access to the account and if there is, cut up the card. It can't be easy to get at, otherwise you may get tempted!

To recap, you need to annihilate your bad debt. That is any debt that is not making you any money – credit cards, personal loans or car finance. Then you have to get into the habit of paying yourself first.

And remember that once you've set a percentage of what you are to pay yourself there is nothing to stop you getting creative with your business so that you make more money. If your business is making $1000 a month then you might pay yourself $100 but there is nothing to stop you getting creative and increasing your profit so you can pay yourself $1000 or $10,000 a month!

The only thing you need to worry about for your savings account is investment skills and how to leverage that money at some point, but for now let's focus on how to make more money in your business.

GET COMPLETELY FREE

'The Financial Rescue Package' E- book

Financial Rescue is written for people who want to get out of debt and create financial success! This powerful little book covers the 5 important areas that you must know to create financial success. These 5 essential areas are the foundation that is used by every successful person. It also gives you 10 very effective tips to help you on the path to financial freedom.

Go now to www.RichesFromBusiness.com/FreeGift

Using Strategies and Structure to Skyrocket Your Success

If you want to be truly successful, then I will give you the formula that I have used for years. It is the same two-part formula that I have imparted to the thousands of people who have come to my seminars around the world. The first part is called Strategies and the second part is called Structure.

Strategies are the actual techniques you need to use. Let's say I wanted to bake a world-class chocolate cake. The first thing I would need to do is go out and buy a recipe book. However, I don't want to bake just any old cake, I want a world-class one. So I go to the local bookstore. As luck would have it, the world famous chef, Antoine Du Pree has just release his new book called 'World-class Chocolate Cakes'. I'm very excited!

I rush home, eager to begin. I open the book and there on page 71 is the masterpiece I've been looking for. It looks extraordinary, my mouth is watering just looking at the picture and I can't wait to begin. I quickly make a note of all the ingredients and go down to the supermarket. Soon I'm cooking up a storm. I follow the recipe in minute detail and before long there is the most amazing aroma coming out of the kitchen. Finally ... the moment I've been waiting for. I pull the cake out of the oven, let it cool and cover it in icing. Standing back to admire my masterpiece I realise ... there is a problem.

What I was after was a world-class chocolate cake. I know Monsieur Du Pree is a world-class chef and I followed his recipe down to the letter. So how is it that my cake doesn't look as good as his? The cake I made is pretty good, in fact, it's bordering on great. But it's not world-class. Why not?

The problem is that Monsieur Du Pree has a different structure than me when it comes to chocolate cakes! Becoming successful is just like baking a cake. You definitely need a great recipe – a plan or series of techniques. But more importantly you need to master the other part of the equation – the structure.

The success structure

The easiest way to explain structure is to imagine two goldfish in a pet shop. One day two sisters, Tanya and Rose, walk into the pet shop and buy the goldfish. Tanya puts her small goldfish into a tiny little bowl. There is just enough room for a few pebbles and a miniature plant.

Rose, however, has a massive aquarium given to her by her Uncle Phil, who is an expert in raising fish. It covers the entire length of one wall in her room. After a few months Tanya walks into Rose's room and is staggered. The goldfish in the aquarium is huge. Perhaps she's mistaken? She runs into her room and checks. Sure enough her little fish is still the same size as when she bought it. Thinking her little fish is sick, she calls Uncle Phil. 'Tanya,' he says, 'There is nothing wrong with your goldfish. The reason it has stayed small is because it is governed by the size of the bowl. Rose's goldfish is bigger because it had more space to grow because she put it in the aquarium.'

Goldfish grow to a size appropriate to the size of their bowl. If the fish bowl is small, the goldfish will remain small. If we put that same goldfish in a bigger bowl, it would grow.

The fishbowl is the structure and you and I are much like those goldfish. Each of us has a structure that we live in. It is made up of a myriad of things including our beliefs, mindsets and habits. What we believe is possible in life is very much dependent on the conditioning we received as children and the environment we grew up in. Thankfully, our ideas can be changed in later life by new experiences and access to new information and knowledge and this allows us to expand that limited goldfish bowl we unconsciously live in.

Returning to my chocolate cake ... I could try five different times to bake that cake and the reality is it would probably never turn out like the master chef's cake. However, if I were able to spend some time with Monsieur Du Pree and learn from him, discover his habits and mindsets, then one day my cake would be a masterpiece – because I would have both the strategies (recipe) and the structure (mindset) to replicate his creation.

The difference between people who are very successful and those who aren't is that they have a different structure. Andrew Carnegie, the wealthy industrialist turned philanthropist, said 'I am no longer cursed by the affliction of poverty because I have taken possession of my own mind.' Carnegie had a far bigger structure or mindset than the average person. He was an extraordinary character and it was he who encouraged Napoleon Hill to dedicate his life to discovering the science of success, resulting, of course, in his famous book. Although Carnegie started his life in poverty in Scotland, his family moved to America and he is responsible for building one of the most powerful and influential corporations in US history. After spending the first part of his life accumulating vast wealth, he spent the last part giving it all away. He established many libraries, schools and universities around the world – so much so that Andrew Carnegie is as famous for his philanthropy as he ever was in business.

Structure is what creates success. Strategies are certainly important but it's your structure that will determine just how far you will go. Let's get a clearer picture of how our structure works. I want you to try a little experiment with me … bring the palms of your hands together and interlace your fingers. Then cross your thumbs. In other words, put one thumb over the top of the other.

Now notice which thumb sits on top of the other. Is it the left or the right? Now, switch thumbs by putting the one that's on the bottom, on the top. How does that feel? For the vast majority of people it usually feels uncomfortable. It's because they have developed a habit and that habit has become part of their structure. For example, people who develop the habit of procrastination miss out on remarkable opportunities. They have developed a 'negative' structure that inhibits their success. Remember Emily from the previous chapter? Somewhere in her structure was an income ceiling of $14 an hour that limited her ability to move past that point – until she understood it.

Your structure is illustrated by the habits you have. Some of those habits, like which thumb crossed which thumb when you clasp your hands together, don't really matter in life. Other habits, such as how much money you think you're worth, can have a huge impact on your results!

Habits are just one part of what forms our structure. Our structure is also created by our beliefs. Let's say someone believes that rich people are crooks, or dishonest. What financial condition do you think this person will be in? Logic would say that if someone identifies rich people as dishonest they won't want to appear dishonest and therefore they are not rich. All my research tells me that those people that complain the loudest about money are the ones who have the least, even though they may secretly covet it. These negative beliefs also help create a 'negative' structure. Our structure is made up of both beliefs and habits. When we change our beliefs and develop powerful new habits, we dramatically increase our ability to succeed.

I remember one occasion when I was leading a seminar, I asked the group, 'What's the difference between someone who makes $100 an hour and someone who makes $1000 an hour?' Quick as a flash, someone yelled out, 'One zero!' The whole room cracked up. Later that night I thought about it and realised that while he was joking, in reality what he was saying was true. It's just a zero. That zero just comes from our structure. If we can learn great strategies and expand our structure to the point that we can use and apply those great strategies, then our lives can change very quickly.

The strategies and structure can be thought of like this … imagine that you are an astronaut and you are strapped into your rocket ship. You can hear the final countdown as your ship prepares to launch for its journey to the moon. You realise that the only thing that is going to get you there is this rocket ship. The announcer continues his count, ' … eight, seven, six …' You're totally focused on your goal – the moon. A few vague doubts rush through your mind. Will the ship be okay? Do you have the skills to navigate the journey? But you remind yourself that it's too late now as you hear, 'One. Ignition. Blast off!' The rocket moves off the ground, the roar is deafening and the speed begins to build. Soon the ground begins to seem a long way away and as you break through the earth's gravitational field it dawns on you that there is absolutely no turning back. You are 100% committed to your goal.

All those late nights of study at command central come flooding back to you and all the complex jargon and mathematical equations become clear, boiling down to a few simple home truths. Basically this rocket ship has two primary sections. The first is the small nose cone where you sit. This is where you punch into the computer the detailed coordinates that will take you to the moon. It is from here that you 'steer' the ship. From here all the strategies that you have learned come into play. However, there is another part of the ship. The rocket ship 'engine' and the fuel tanks are the structure. If you want to pilot your own success rocket ship then you need cutting edge strategies combined with an optimum structure.

I think it's only fair at this point to take a closer look at structure in terms of beliefs. What you believe has a very real and tangible affect on what you experience. Your beliefs are developed over time and, for the most part, they will remain subconscious. In other words, unless someone asks you a direct question – like the question I asked Emily about how much money she was worth – you may never actually become aware of what you believe.

As a result of this unconscious element, beliefs and the importance of beliefs have been hijacked by the personal development industry. There are a lot of people who are into the idea that all they've got to do is visualise – and they'll be rich. So they sit in a chair for 30 minutes a day first thing in the morning and last thing at night and think happy thoughts about the money pouring in. They visualise themselves as a rich person and put up countless laminated cards in their shower and on their fridge about being Ritchie Rich, Rich, Rich. They fill books with goals they want to achieve and the money target they are aiming at and somehow that's all they need to do and everything they dream of will materialise, as if by magic.

I'm really sorry to burst your bubble again but if that's all you do, then not much will happen! Yes, all of those steps can be really useful in working out what you want to achieve and having a clear picture in your mind of your destination, but you need to actually do something in between the visualisation sessions. Spending one hour a day visualising wealth while spending the remaining 23 hours sleeping, playing video games or watching TV isn't going to help you get rich. Spending one hour a day visualising wealth while spending the remaining 23 looking after your health and building your business – that's a different story.

The first idea is delusional. Visualisation is incredibly powerful. Its ability to improve health and assist in healing is well-documented. The connection between increased brain activity and creativity is being proven through a combination of science and eastern philosophy. So I am in no way disparaging visualisation as a tool for helping to materialise your thoughts. But its power is greatly diminished if that's all you do. Thought without action is inert – even really concentrated thought like visualisation! Einstein said, 'Nothing happens until something moves.'

You have to move! You have to get out of your chair and make it happen. You have to get creative in your business and stay committed. You have to be determined to persevere no matter what and you have to be willing to fail, learn and try again. You have to learn to adapt to the signals of success and make shifts in your course so that you arrive at the destination you have been visualising in the armchair in the morning!

You can't just do it metaphysically. I don't care if you sit in a cave in the Himalayas for the rest of your life, wrapped in an orange robe and chanting about the materialisation of gold bars. It's not going to happen. Visualisation is a great strategy and it can really help you to expand your structure but you still need to do something. You have to get into action and make it happen!

The Four Attributes Required to Master Money

The strategies are the easy bit. I'll get to them soon enough but the difference that makes the difference is your structure. If you are living in a little goldfish bowl then you're just not going to grow that big. You're not going to swim in an ocean of wealth until you can jump out of the bowl and expand your structure.

Albert Einstein talked about the boundary conditions of our thinking. Basically, what he was saying is that we are not limited by life – what is possible or impossible is not set by the universe – but set by our own individual perception. We are limited by the boundaries we create. What we believe is possible becomes the walls of the box we live inside. That box is your structure and most people rarely venture outside unless they make a concerted effort to do so.

This chapter looks more closely at how you can master

your structure and create a limitless future for yourself.

Silence the inner critic

Do you have a 'scumbag voice'? If you don't know, I'll save you some time – you do. We all have two voices – one that is positive and encouraging and the other is what I call the 'scumbag voice'. This is the little voice that eats away at your self-confidence and it is your inner critic. It's the one that sniggers when you tell yourself you're going to be rich. It's the one that says, 'Not you, scumbag. Everybody else will be rich except you.'

Don't be too concerned about this voice. Everyone has one. It's just a matter of learning how to turn the volume down or preferably hit the mute button.

Without going into the technicalities of how this voice is developed, suffice to say it is a product of learning and most adults have this voice. If you don't want your children to suffer from it, make a point of encouraging them more than criticising them. Point out their good attributes and make a fuss of their successes rather than always picking on their faults. Encourage them to learn from mistakes and separate the mistake or outcome from them as a human being. Just because someone fails an exam doesn't make them a failure.

As we learn, we fail. That's how we learn and yet as an adult failure is no longer acceptable so we beat ourselves up for not getting it right and the 'scumbag voice' inside has a field day!

Newsflash: IF YOU WANT TO BE RICH, YOU BETTER
GET USED TO FAILING!

I know what it's like to have had failures.

I remember the day like it was riveted to my mind. It was
a cold, brisk day as I skied up to the sign that screamed,
'Warning, Extreme Terrain – Experts Only'. I looked at
the sign and jumped on the lift heading into an area where
people have died – the north face of Crested Butte, the most
extreme, steep terrain of any ski resort in North America. The
question went through my mind, 'Am I really ready for this?'
I looked around, the snow was still coming down and it was
already knee-deep on the ground. This was the place I had
been thinking of for three years after the catastrophe.

As the lift ascended into swirling snow and pine trees,
my mind drifted back three years. The doctors had assured
me it was a normal operation to replace the ligament in my
knee. They told me I would be up and around in a matter of
weeks. However, fate had something else in mind. To this
day no one really knows how it happened but I developed a
rare condition immediately after the operation called a reflex
sympathetic dystrophy that switched off all the impulses to
my leg, effectively rendering it dead. I was on crutches for
eight months; I lost so much strength that I did not have the
ability to lift a suitcase into the back of the car or to perform
normal day-to-day functions. I felt 90 years old. My body lost
all ability to perform the simple task of walking – it simply
did not have the strength to do it and it had forgotten how.
I went to every medico, sports doctor, physio and natural

healer that I could find. There were people who wondered if I would ever be able to walk again. However, in the back of my mind I set myself a goal. I wanted to ski the extreme terrain of the north face. At times the goal seemed ridiculous because I could not walk more than 100 metres on crutches before I felt worn out. I was someone who had been really fit before the operation and now was unable to walk! However, I kept going and one day I found someone who finally turned on the impulses in my leg and I began to walk – it was a year before I could walk properly again. And then, endless months and months of rehabilitation.

As the lift arrived at the top I came back to the present, here I was – at the top of the north face. I skied around the bend in the early morning light and the blowing snow, and stood on top of this vast expanse where there was only one way to go – down. Falling was not an option. It was outrageously steep – off the charts – and went down for hundreds of metres. As I looked down, I thought, 'This is what all the training is for,' and launched myself off the lip and into the abyss. The first thought was to ignore the instincts of the body to sit back – that's deadly – as I would be unbalanced and almost certainly fall. Forcing myself to keep my upper body straight down the hill, all I could see was the light dry powder snow pluming around me, coming up in giant sprays and the quiet 'shush, shush' as my skis came around beneath me. And then my mind went blank as I became lost in the moment, sailing down the mountain, not another soul in sight and then the joy building and exploding as I let out a huge scream, 'Whhhooooooo'. I soaked in the moment and thanked God for the privilege of being in that wild place. I skied nearly all day and came home with a smile from ear to ear and glowing like a Christmas tree.

Anyone who achieves anything worthwhile in life did so because they tried and failed and got back up and tried something new until it worked. One of the most destructive ideas that exists in our society is the concept of failure and success. Everything is set up for success even though success is impossible without failure. No one wants to talk about that bit though. It's not sexy or exciting or interesting so it's brushed under the carpet.

When I make a mistake I try and give myself one quick punch to the head to wake myself up. I assess the situation to find out what happened and what I can learn and then I move on. You need to have that moment of truth. You definitely need to be truthful about your role in the mistake, but don't wallow in it.

Let's say your living room at home is a mess and you decide it's about time you cleaned it up ... with your eyes closed. Would you be able to clean the room? No. You need to be able to see everything that's in the room in order to properly clean it up. It's the same with mistakes or failure. Often it's so painful that we don't want to look at the error. It's easier to turn our back and pretend it didn't happen. We instinctively want to close our eyes and get out of the situation as quickly as possible.

But if you do that it's like trying to clean up a mess with your eyes closed. You have to open your eyes, get the torch out and shine some light into the situation so you can find out what really went wrong. Was it you? Was it someone else? Was there fault or misunderstanding on all sides? What could you have done differently that would have stopped the failure from happening? Could that be implemented next time? Only by really getting into the failure and ferreting around in it – with your eyes and your mind wide open – will you get some solutions.

I know it's a cliché but it's a cliché for a reason – a failure is only a failure when you don't learn anything from it! So pay attention to the failures as well as the successes and learn from everything.

The scumbag voice is a dream killer. If you listen it will scare you into playing it safe and remaining comfortable. Robert Frost described the dream killer when he said, 'Something we were withholding made us weak, until we found out that it was ourselves.'

We often tend to think that those who have become successful have done so because they had no doubts or they were lucky. Yet the statistics speak for themselves. The Beatles were turned down by ten recording studios before EMI finally picked them up. Richard Bach was rejected 18 times before someone finally decided to publish Jonathon Livingston Seagull. I think my favourite, 'against all odds' story is that of Walt Disney, who was turned down by 321 banks before someone finally said yes to his dream – Disneyland.

When you read the works of many of these people they all speak about having to face their fears and doubts. They had to turn and look their own dream killer square in the eye and banish it time and again as they moved toward their goal.

It is important to realise that this is only a small part of you. Who you really are is so extraordinary it would blow your mind. Rumi said, 'When you see your true beauty, you will be the idol of yourself.' And this is a fact. Always keep in mind your extraordinary potential. You are an amazing being. So keep the fires of your dream fully alight.

I'd encourage you to look inside. However, do not let the scumbag voice get the better of you. You have to believe in yourself. Here is how you handle the scumbag voice – you simply do not listen. If you had an enemy who followed you around all day telling you negative things about yourself – what would happen if you refused to listen? Eventually they would get bored and go pester someone else! And that is how you handle the scumbag voice – refuse to listen!! Do not give it any energy!

Your scumbag voice is just a little voice inside your head. It's perfectly normal and you're not going nuts, so don't worry. But you are nuts if you listen to it. It's your own voice! It's just a pessimistic, negative part of your personality but it's not WHO YOU ARE. It has no power unless you agree with it.

Remember your scumbag voice only has power to limit your dreams and steal your confidence if you let it. Don't listen. That's the key, don't listen. Most people think that's too simple but it is usually the simple things in life that make the biggest difference. If you continually ignored a schoolyard bully he or she would eventually find someone else to annoy. Even if you have to pretend to ignore that person and remain poker-faced eventually they'll get frustrated at not having any effect and go away. The scumbag voice is the same. Just hit an imaginary 'delete' button in your mind and get on with being successful. As you get more practised at this you will be surprised to find that you hear it less and less, until eventually it's just a little murmur from your past.

Apply the 'Avargo principle' at all times

This is the secret I call 'Avargo'. It is so powerful that I actually named a company after it. Avargo can create financial wealth. Avargo was the secret that I used to write my first book, which became a bestseller. When I first came up with the idea of writing a book, the obstacles just seemed completely insurmountable. For starters I couldn't type. I mean I couldn't even tap with two fingers. Not only that, I wasn't a natural writer, I'd get bored too quickly and my mind went faster than my fingers! But I put Avargo into practice – I got a typing program and I took a course in writing. And I wrote the book. Two major publishers told me later on that it was an extremely well written book and I never thought of myself as a writer and I can sure as heck tell you that my old school teachers didn't either.

So I kept moving forward and I kept applying Avargo. After the book was written we decided to self-publish it. Everybody thought that we were crazy. The howls of derision were deafening. Do you know the odds of a self-published book ever making it, everybody said. Are you crazy? But we went ahead anyway. Everybody said we would never stand a chance against the big publishing houses. We didn't know anything about publishing but we decided to follow our instincts and use the Avargo principle. So my wife and I opened up our own publishing house and we called it Avargo Press and when the book hit several bestseller lists many people were dumbfounded and it was later picked up by one of the world's biggest publishers who went on to take the book even further.

So by now you are probably wondering what Avargo is! Well, in Australia there is a very common saying, in fact, it is part of the cultural slang. You hear it screamed out by spectators in sporting stadiums. It is three words – 'have a go' – and if you say it very fast with an Australian accent it sounds like 'av ar go.' Considering we really didn't know what we were doing it seemed like the perfect name for the business – Avargo. So the next time you have a dream or some deep intuitive feeling to do something, just think Avargo. Avargo is essential because the law of action is all about getting into motion. You must be in motion. You have to get off your backside and Av A Go!

One of my students really took this idea to heart and proved just how powerful it is. Daniel Fenech was just 20 years old when he first came to one of my Entrepreneur's seminars two years ago. He didn't know a thing about business. However, what he did have was a ton of enthusiasm and the desire to learn. At the time Daniel was a frustrated employee of a drama school. He knew he had a lot of potential but felt he was restricted in his ability to use it. So Daniel decided to do something very courageous – he started his own drama school. He then realised he needed some expertise so he joined my inner circle coaching program.

Now the interesting thing about Daniel is that when you give him a good idea, he acts on it. On my inner circle coaching program I gave him some 'out of the box' Financial Acceleration $uccess Strategies (FA$T). Low cost, specific strategies that produce big results – some of which I'll be sharing with you very soon. He never procrastinated, he never questioned the advice or made any assumptions about whether suggestions would work or not, he just acted on them. The first thing he did was approach the owner of a building to see if he would give him some floor space, rent-free. Now some people would say, 'Wow this kid is pretty dumb, who is going to give him that?' Except that he got it. Not only did he get the floor space, the owner of the building promoted him too – at no cost. He applied the Avargo principle and made things happen.

His next problem was that he had no money for insurance. Undaunted, he wrote a letter to a local community foundation requesting the amount for the insurance premium. Once again he got the money – at no cost. Using some of the techniques I showed him he was able to go out and get over $9,000 of free publicity and insurance. He's now on his way to becoming a very successful entrepreneur at the ripe old age of 22.

So what was Daniel's strategy? First, he recognised that he needed to get some help and education and someone recommended that he go to one of my events. He then recognised that my inner circle program could give him the mentorship he was after. Next – he acted on that information. He never thought like the 'herd', nor did he make any assumptions about what might happen – he just did it. He thought like a maverick. And most importantly, he asked. If you don't ask, the answer is already no, so just by asking the question you automatically increase you chances of a 'yes' by 50%.

(If you are interested in finding more about any of the programs I run, check out **www.RichesFromBusiness.com**).

In business we so often shoot ourselves in the foot because we don't implement our ideas. In a meeting someone may suggest something really clever and suddenly a cacophony of input will result in the idea being scrapped. People will say, 'Yeah, but he'll never agree to that'. Or 'Well, that might have worked in Melbourne but it won't work here'. The fact is you don't know what someone will say unless you ask them. You don't know if it will work outside Melbourne unless you try it. But their assumptions influence the outcome because if someone doesn't think that a person will agree to something, they don't ask properly. They expect rejection and sure enough that's exactly what they get. If they try a strategy they do so half-heartedly so they can smugly say, 'I told you so'. It's crazy – you're unconsciously creating failure so you can be 'right' about your assumptions. You're confirming your failure without ever really trying.

You will probably have heard of a placebo – a sugar pill or saline solution that is given to a patient who is told that it is medicine. In many studies these placebos have been shown to have as much, if not more, effect that the actual drug.

Traditionally that has been put down to the patient's trust and faith in the doctor. But in a bizarre twist it has been shown that the attitude of the doctor administering the placebo may also play a part. In California, a placebo specialist tells the story of a doctor treating an asthma patient who was having trouble breathing. The doctor gave the patient a sample of a new potent drug and within minutes the patient showed spectacular improvement. However, the next time the patient had a severe attack his doctor decided to try a placebo to see how much of his patient's attack was psychosomatic. This time the patient did not respond and complained that there must have been something wrong with the new drug. Naturally the doctor assumed that the new drug must indeed be a valid asthma medication until he received a letter from the drug manufacturer apologising for accidentally sending him a placebo! The only explanation of this was that the doctor had been unconsciously more enthusiastic about the treatment when he thought it was a real drug than when he thought it was a placebo.

Although fascinating from a medical perspective, this happens all the time. We infect our results with our preconceived assumptions. For example, Daniel didn't know whether the people he was going to ask for help were going to say yes or no. He didn't have any preconceived prejudices about the likelihood of success. All he knew was that he was going to ask and try to convey his desire and passion for the project so that he would positively infect those he sought help from. And it worked. All too often we make decisions about what others are going to say that pollute the outcome.

Just like the doctor. The only difference between the 'drug' that worked and the 'drug' that didn't was his attitude.

It's the same in business – first you have to ask – and just as importantly you have to expect to get a yes!

Why don't people take action?

I'm not going to spend too much time on the reasons people don't act, because the list is endless. Suffice to say that we have two types of fear. The first is what I call healthy fear. Now to describe healthy fear I would like you to imagine standing on a plane – just near the door of a plane, without a parachute, and you're about to jump. That would be healthy fear because if anything went wrong and you slipped, you're going to die – simple as that! That sort of fear keeps us alive and away from aeroplane doors without parachutes.

There is, however, another kind of fear and it's unhealthy fear. It's the preoccupation with things that might happen in the future. If we spend too much time worrying about the future it destroys our today. Most of what you worry about won't even happen anyway. Some bright spark once said that fear was actually an acronym for false, evidence, appearing, real. It might be a little cheesy, but it's actually very true!

At the end of the day, fear is a cop-out for most people. The fact that most people don't do what they know they should do, or suspect they could do, is because they don't want to stand out. Most people are more interested in belonging.

In his ground-breaking book, Influence, Dr Robert

Cialdini illustrated how there are six basic yet powerful principles of psychology that direct human behaviour. They are:

- Reciprocity
- Consistency
- Social proof
- Authority
- Scarcity
- Liking

Social proof is the one most relevant to us here because individuals use social proof to decide what is acceptable for them. They will scan the environment and if other people they consider similar to themselves are doing something, or buying something, then this will unconsciously influence their acceptance of it. Huge companies will often conduct psychographic studies to determine the hidden emotional drivers that make people buy a product. It turns out that the number one driver in western society is 'I want to belong'.

One of the biggest fears we have is the fear of ostracism, or being cast out. Success therefore brings with it an inherent separation. Is it any wonder therefore that people are terrified to stand out? Being singled out is a scary thing for most people and is probably why speaking in public is considered so terrifying.

There are countless people who are so subconsciously frightened of being criticised that they limit themselves from ever pursuing their potential – which is pretty stupid when you think about it! You can't ever control how others will see you anyway so you have to be honest with yourself and if that means that you want to be rich then step up to the plate and take responsibility for that dream.

You can't waver on your commitments for success – you're either in or out. There is no middle ground and you will stand out. You don't have to drive around in a Ferrari if you don't want to, but you will stand out as being different. So get over it!

So many people think it's better to sit on the fence and pretend that, 'If it wasn't for X, I could have been rich'. I don't care what or who your X is – it's just an excuse. It's certainly safe if you never Avargo and you'll get to the end of your days without many scary moments. But you're also liable to get to the end of your days full of regret and self-pity and that's not what you deserve. Hey, it may be that you give it your best shot and it doesn't work out, but isn't that better than some cop-out about how you couldn't even try? The thing is that if you do apply the Avargo principle you'll be astonished at how far it will take you.

When you fully understand that you can't control whether people will like you or not, or whether they will criticise you or not, or whether you will fail or not, you stop worrying. Because none of it really matters – if you are doing the best you can, caring for the people you love in your life and you are not doing anything that keeps you awake at night, then just get on with it. Enjoy it, and embrace the opportunities that life can offer. I promise you it creates an incredible sense of freedom when you live life on your own terms. Remember there is a power in you that wants you to be all that you can be – give it wings.

It's worth noting before we leave this topic that Cialdini's principle of consistency can also play a part in stopping people from taking action and changing things. Consistency is the innate need we have to remain consistent with previous decisions.

Say, for example, a business makes a strategic choice and runs full tilt toward that choice. The more resources they throw at it, and the more time and energy they spend on it, the more committed to it they become, regardless of whether or not it's working. We need to be right, and rather than stop and admit we were wrong and change direction, we actually throw more weight behind it. It's a crazy way to do things but it's a very strong driver and you need to understand how it plays out. Instead of backing off and changing tack, they spend increasing time justifying their original decisions. Some major businesses have done this with spectacular results.

Motorola spent billions on a satellite phone system, for example, and despite continued losses and countless analysts insisting they should shut it down, it took years and billions in losses before they finally came to their senses. They were so hell-bent on remaining consistent with their original vision that they couldn't see that the market didn't exist. Or if they saw it, they didn't want to accept it.

Don't get too rigid, and take your ego out of play. Follow the money. Not the ego!

Know the difference between rules and laws

The next prerequisite from mastering your structure is learning to differentiate between rules and laws.

Laws are what govern our society and they are there to protect people and make the world a better place. They ensure that people behave morally and ethically or at least that's the principle. Rules, on the other hand, are guidelines. If you break a rule no one is going to throw you in jail!

The problem is that most people have a whole bunch of laws in their head that don't exist. Or they have a bunch of rules that they believe are laws and that limits their structure of what's possible.

Looking back to Cialdini's principles of psychology, authority and liking are important in this context. We are taught from a young age to obey the rules. At school we get into trouble if we don't and nothing changes much in adulthood. For some, the need to be liked is so strong that we won't go against the grain anyway. It's too uncomfortable to even bend the rules. But there is much more going on than that. Our innate need to obey people in authority is quite scary. Just look at the influence a man in a white coat has. We are so ingrained to believe that the doctor knows best that we are quite happy to go along with whatever he or she suggests. As I mentioned earlier, the effect of the placebo is often put down to the belief the patient has in a cure or in the doctor and this facilitates the healing, despite no drug or intervention actually having occurred! Many studies into this phenomenon have proven that our respect for authority and the trust we have in our physician can have a huge influence – good and bad – on our recovery.

Basically we are hard-wired to obey authority and follow the rules.

And that might be fine for some people, but seriously, do you think someone like Richard Branson obeys the rules of business, or does he write his own rules as he goes along?

In order to be really successful in business you have to separate laws from rules. Laws must be adhered to and you wouldn't want to break the law anyway. But all the rules about how your business should look and what success will look like – scrap them all. Remember Sarah from Chapter 5? Her rules said that a successful business needed to have premises and an office full of staff. Who made that a rule? Business has to make money and the best way to make money is to give the market something it wants and values. Apart from that – there is no formula. When Sarah was able to see that her rules about business were making her unhappy and poorer than she could have been, she sold the premises and created a business on her terms.

You can do anything that you want and that's what an entrepreneur does. They think outside the square. As John Paul Getty said, and he certainly knew a thing or two about wealth, 'You don't get rich by being a conformist. You have to think outside the square.'

Understand commitment and apply it

Understanding commitment is an extension of a greater

understanding of the snap point that we talked about in Chapter 2. In the seminars that I run on making more money in your business, we usually have a full house. It's obvious that there is a real and genuine need for the material I'm presenting because these programs are consistently full.

But the commitment of those who attend is like chalk and cheese ...

Interested

First, there are those who are 'interested' in making more money from their business. Often people at this stage won't even have a business! But they are interested in the concept. They may be in a job they dislike and are casting their net out into the world to see what alternatives there are.

Many years ago I was asked to be a guest speaker at a wealth creation program. I entered the room and everyone was hyped. The atmosphere was really positive and I could tell that everyone was excited about the possibility of being wealthy. But it didn't feel quite right to me.

As I came on stage I was welcomed by a sea of eager faces all intent on hearing whatever pearls of wisdom I would impart! I opened by asking the audience what the program was all about. We were half-way through the event and they were all pretty vocal about being interactive and several voices roared out, 'To create wealth and have financial independence.'

I said that I certainly couldn't argue with that and asked, 'So how many of you are committed to being wealthy and financially independent?' Every hand in the room shot up.

Now I've told this story before and it's even in my first book but I'm repeating it here because it's really important. I could have easily moved on to the body of my presentation and certainly that's what most presenters on wealth would have done. After all, it's all about giving the audience what they want. But I don't always agree with that. It's also about helping the audience understand what it is they really want and giving them real ways to achieve that. Not just hot air and promises.

Anyway, I repeated the question. Once more all the hands went up, this time even more vigorously than before. I kept repeating the question over and over and I think a few people started to wonder if I was senile or something! There were certainly plenty of puzzled faces in the crowd as people started to get agitated.

Finally, a big Polynesian who was sitting at the back of the room rose to speak. He was literally a mountain of a man and commanded an incredible presence. The room hushed as he stood there. He looked directly at me and said, 'Brendan, I thought I was extremely committed but you've got me thinking. The truth is what means more to me than anything is family. I've always wanted more money but I've never really committed to it.'

I looked at him and said, 'That's okay. At least now you know what you are committed to.' Every person in the room got a chance to speak. At the end of the night there were two people in that group who, beyond a shadow of a doubt were committed to financial independence. Guess what? Those two were already financially independent.

Wanting to have something, hoping that one day you might be rich, will not make you rich. Now it may be that, like my Polynesian friend, you may work out that your family is actually more important but at least you'll know what's real for you. And perhaps you can learn to accommodate both. Use your love of your family to drive you toward riches. It doesn't have to be an either/or situation but you do need to make the goal of making more money a serious commitment.

If you're interested in it – it's still a choice. And that is not a commitment.

External commitment

The next level of commitment is external commitment. It can help you get things done but it's not the powerhouse commitment you need to have if you are going to be rich. It's based on external factors when you are committed to something because it's expected or wanted by someone else.

For example, I know businesspeople who would swear they never operate from external commitment. One friend of mine had a company who employed 47 staff in a landmark building. This company won one of the most prestigious business awards in Australia and was featured on television as a 'success story'. They certainly looked successful yet they weren't making any real profit. One day the owner woke up and realised that he was operating in the classic, 'big is better' syndrome and his motivation was coming from 'looking like a success'. He took a giant axe to the business, regained his peace of mind and increased profitability.

External commitments can also occur when someone just can't say no. They agree to things requested by other people and then feel angry about it afterwards. The best way to solve this one is to understand your success drivers better and have a clear idea of what you are trying to achieve. Then when people ask you to do things you have a very clear guide to work from. Either you agree because you want to help that person or you agree because it marries well with your own objectives. Either is fine but be conscious about what you're doing and if the request falls into neither camp then say 'No'.

If you think about it like cause and effect, then external commitment is all about effect. You are affected by other people's opinions or requests. Or you are affected by external events and circumstances that you may not have much control over. Internal commitment, which we will talk about next, is all about moving to the cause side of the equation. This is when you take charge of your destiny and plot your own course regardless of others, and regardless of the events that may arrive to bump you off course.

External commitment is still better than no commitment at all and it's certainly more powerful that mild interest and dreams of 'someday I'm going to be rich', but it's best to use it as a springboard into internal commitment.

Internal commitment

This is getting much closer to real commitment. At this stage you are your own judge and jury. This is a level of commitment where you operate at your highest level of performance. It is based on the satisfaction of knowing that you went to your own personal limit and did what you really wanted to do.

You've got a plan and you're in action working toward your dreams. Often this type of commitment occurs at the snap point. Something happens and you just can't take it any more. A renewed level of determination and drive for change overtakes you and things start to turn around. Most people will never get to this level of commitment without some serious wake-up call!

But when they do, they achieve a tremendous sense of freedom and independence. They are free to decide their own journey and live by the rules they make up, not someone else's. They are not trying to live up to someone else's expectations. Instead they are dancing to their own beat and setting their own goals.

Once you harness this internal commitment you become much more your own person. Moving from external commitment to internal commitment can be a bold and courageous step because there is a fear that you will be disliked or abandoned. And yet to do anything else is to abandon yourself and your own dreams.

Totality

The final stage on the commitment journey is totality. Totality is where the mission becomes more important than the person on the mission. It is the realm where you go way beyond what you considered possible. Everything extraneous vanishes from your field of vision and nothing else matters but achieving your intention.

This is where corporations are born, great causes are supported and visions are realised. It's no longer about an individual and his or her goals – it's much bigger than that. And will probably move forward with or without you!

Whether it is in your career, your relationship, or your spiritual life, totality has the power to let you soar with the eagles.

When you operate in a spirit of totality you command attention just by your very presence. There is something about people that are living full tilt. It's almost magnetic and they invariably exude a rock-solid and unwavering focus. They emanate a sense of certainty.

Bottom line is you have to be committed and that is the fourth aspect of structure that you must master if you are to achieve wealth. You must be committed. Absolutely committed. You have to make an internal decision that you're going to make money before you make it. It is the very first principle of the money attraction formula. The root of the word decide actually means to 'cut off from'. A true decision cuts you off from any alternative route – it is a verbal commitment to that choice.

Sometimes you've got to put the cart before the horse. You've got to be committed before the horse can even show up. You've got to decide beyond any shadow of a doubt that you are going to achieve what you set out to achieve. It's a resolution set in stone. There can be no part of you that does not make the decision; you have to be congruent and fully aligned to that outcome.

And when you are, strange things will happen. As Goethe said, 'Whatever you can do, or dream you can, begin it. Boldness has genius, power, and magic in it'. And there really is magic in it. Strange forces that we still don't understand seem to conspire to help us achieve our deepest commitments. Buckminster Fuller, one of the great geniuses of the 20th century said something similar: 'The principles will be revealed upon the decision'.

Don't worry about the how just yet. Just get clear about the why first. (Don't worry I will be showing you some really powerful 'how' principles a little later.) The plan will form once the decision and commitment is made.

I have a great story about a friend of mine that illustrates this perfectly. She had only been in Sydney for a few months and was feeling a little unsure of her next best step. Recently emigrated, she was, for want of a better word, 'lost'. Over the course of a couple of weeks she kept seeing advertisements for a certain up-coming seminar. It would be mentioned in conversations, and a series of synchronicities led her to attend the seminar. By the end of the weekend she had committed to paying a serious amount of money to attend a series of seminars around the world. I've asked her what the best thing she learnt from that experience and she replied, 'Although I got a lot out of the training and met some great people the really amazing thing I learnt was the power of a real decision. I'd heard quotes like Goethe's before but I didn't really appreciate how true it is. When you really decide something, and I mean really commit to making something happen, something incredible happens and it's like magic. All the obstacles that would have stopped you if you'd considered them just melt away.' Having recently emigrated to Australia she didn't have the money to make that commitment and yet within a few weeks her boss said he was so impressed with her investment in her education that he was going to pay for half the training. Money from an unexpected source came through and several months later the seminar company offered her a discount. In the end she didn't borrow a cent to do the courses or for the two international airfares and 5-star accommodation! Following the courses, and as a direct result of that investment, she was offered her dream job with a salary increase of $25,000! There is magic in commitment -real, inexplicable magic.

GET COMPLETELY FREE

'Create a Stampede of New Business and Profits'

The 10 rules of the successful entrepreneur. A powerful 10 day course on discovering the tools to turn yourself into a highly successful entrepreneur.

Go now to www.RichesFromBusiness.com/FreeGift

CHAPTER 12

Beware the Monkey and How It Can Destroy Your Success!

So far we've looked at how it's important to make money a priority if you want to make more in your business. And while that certainly means you have to focus on delivering something the market wants and is willing to pay for, the most important step is to ensure that 'making money' is in your top 3 priority list. We've talked about how you must annihilate any personal debt and get into the habit of paying yourself first. And we've talked about strategies and structure. The strategies relate to the things that you will do in your business. These are important because you just have to get into action and try things. You have to cast aside your preconceptions and just make your dreams come true. Visualising that you're going to get rich in between watching TV shows isn't going to work. We've also discussed the importance of structure and how you must consciously learn to expand your structure, put those preconceptions aside and think bigger. Get out of the little goldfish bowl and swim in a much bigger ocean.

If you do all these things then you are really making progress toward your goal. But there is one thing that could trip you up ... especially if you don't know it's coming. Beware the monkeys!

In an experiment to study behaviour, scientists put four monkeys in a large enclosure. As a quick aside I don't agree with this experiment but I think it is incredibly representative of human nature. In the middle of the enclosure there was a tall wooden pole with a bunch of bananas on the top. The monkeys couldn't shake them off and needed to climb the pole to get the bananas. It wasn't long before the first monkey went to climb the pole to retrieve the prize. Only, the monkey was blasted with a high pressure water hose, as part of the experiment. Every time any one of the monkeys made an attempt to climb the pole and retrieve the bananas they would get hosed. While the water didn't hurt them it was obviously very unpleasant. At this point in the experiment they stopped using the hose but none of the monkeys made any attempt to climb the pole.

They then removed one of the original monkeys and added a new monkey into the enclosure. Of course this new monkey spotted the bananas and went to climb the pole. And that's when it got interesting. All three of the remaining original monkeys tried to pull the new monkey off the pole. Soon even the new monkey stopped trying to climb the pole and he hadn't even experienced the water hose. Eventually they kept replacing all the monkeys. None of these monkeys had ever been hosed down but all of them reacted the same way, none of them would make any attempt to go up the pole. Every time a new monkey was brought into the cage the existing monkeys would stop it from going up the pole to retrieve the bananas.

In human beings, particularly in the Australian and New Zealand cultures, this is called the 'tall poppy syndrome'. It exists everywhere, only it's so pervasive here we actually have a name for it.

Remember earlier we talked about how important it was for people to belong. This is an extension of this. Now the original monkeys may have pulled the new monkey off the pole so he didn't have to experience the discomfort of the high pressure water hose, and certainly there will be people in your life that do the same. As soon as you declare your intention to change and commit to making more money in your business there will be people in your life who will try to stop you climbing the pole. In their mind they will be helping you or trying to protect you from failure, and this may even be true, but you can't let it stop you reaching your bananas!

Human beings want to belong and as soon as you appear to change your friends and family may start to feel uncomfortable. Before you changed your focus you were probably all much the same. There was a camaraderie and similarity between you that was not threatening. But as soon as you alter that dynamic, you not only disturb the equilibrium but you also disturb them individually. It unconsciously makes them assess what they are doing with their life – and if they don't like the answer you can guarantee that you will be getting the blame.

In my experience if you want to know how far someone is going to go up the pole in quest of bananas, just look at the monkeys or friends they surround themselves with. If their friends are committed to getting the bananas then they will be too. However, people that surround themselves with friends who always play it safe are likely to play exactly the same game.

Now I've got friends that have no money and I have friends that are multi-millionaires many times over. The friends that have no money often still play a big game in their own way, either in a sporting area or maybe in a spiritual area or philanthropic arena. Whatever it is, they don't care about my money or their lack of it because they are living their life the way they want. You see it's not about the money. It's about having the courage to live life on your own terms.

Most people in the world don't do that, so when they meet someone that does – especially if it's you and you guys used to hang out together – that can be very uncomfortable. Because they know you, they can't brush it off and assume that you must have been really well educated, or had connections or had money to start with. They know in their heart of hearts that they are actually just like you only you've got off your backside and made something of your life and perhaps they haven't. And that can be hard to take. So instead of receiving the encouragement and support you expected you'll be ridiculed. People will criticise you and assume you've changed!

I know when I started to make serious money, people who knew me when I was broke would make little comments like,

'Oh I see you're on TV again', or 'I heard you in the radio AGAIN!' I certainly didn't hear much by way of support or congratulations when I went out and bought my first Porsche.

Recently at a seminar, a participant lamented that since becoming a successful businesswoman, some of her friends felt uncomfortable around her. A friend of mine, who is one of the world's leading impressionist painters, also told me that while some people love his success, others feel uncomfortable or resentful. Even though he really struggled for years to make a living, never mind becoming rich.

I call this phenomenon 'splitting the world'. Whenever you decide to do something extraordinary, stand out from the crowd or become successful, you draw a line down the middle of the world. People will take three positions in regard to your success. The first position is those that stand on the line, they are the people who don't care what you are doing. The second position is on your side of the line. These are the people that will encourage and support you and your dreams. And the third position is for those on the other side of the line. These are people who will not support you, either through silence or active criticism. These are the people who don't want you to succeed – and sadly they are rarely strangers.

Many people deliberately or subconsciously limit their success because they want to be accepted. They know if they stand out they will 'split the world'. You see humans crave love above all other emotions. Love is essential to our wellbeing. When babies are left in orphanages, without being touched, they develop a condition called mirasma, which can be fatal. Lack of love and affection is very damaging and so our desire to maintain connection is powerful, even if it's not that helpful.

However, there is a big difference between love and acceptance. If you deliberately or subconsciously limit your success, because you want to be accepted, then you are choosing acceptance over the life you truly want. Remember, all those who achieved greatness overcame opposition. Even Einstein said that most of his opposition came from mediocre minds.

I'm not saying stop hanging around with your old friends, and certainly you can't walk away from your family, but I would suggest you become aware of how others make you feel. If you find that you always feel deflated when you are around a certain person then simply limit your contact. You can't afford to be around other people's scumbag voice as well as your own! Try to expand your circle to include like-minded people so you can bounce ideas around in a supportive environment. Try to mix with people that are even more successful than you as this will help you to raise your game too. It might feel uncomfortable for you at first but that's because you're expanding your structure and that can feel weird sometimes!

Also, I'd advise that you keep your plans quiet at the start. Don't go broadcasting how you're going to be rich. Just make your commitments and do it. Actions always speak louder than words anyway.

So what's the remedy? Just don't worry about what anyone thinks of you. What someone else thinks of you is none of your business. Commit today to focus on the life you truly want and achieve your dreams and personal greatness.

The Seven Deadly Sins of Time – How to Work a Couple of Days a Week

Okay, do you want to know some of the secrets to having more time and more money? Just say yes, because we are about to cover some really powerful stuff! Here are some of the tricks I use that make me more productive and free up my time.

There is one thing that we all have in common. It doesn't matter where you live, what colour your skin is, what religion you believe in or how much money you have in the bank – we all have 24 hours in a day.

When I sat with my head in my hands wondering how on earth I was going to support my family in a business that made no money I inadvertently discovered something. In reaching my own personal 'snap point' I changed my focus from working like a dog for nothing to making the most amount of money in the shortest amount of time with the least amount of effort. You should make this your mantra, 'the most amount of money in the shortest amount of time with the least amount of effort'. As I said in Chapter 2, NET PROFIT was my only objective. When I say net profit here is what I mean – ACIP.

Actual
Cash
In
Pocket

An accountant will tell you that net profit contains future payments that are on the books but in the real world, 'it ain't cash baby until it's in your pocket'. It needs to be ACIP.

How do you achieve this wondrous state? It meant focusing most of my time (and for you – your time) at the Nexus Point...

I am about to give you a HUGE tip.

The Nexus Point is a secret only known to a small percentage of people AND they are the ones that make the money. If you really grasp this point your life can radically change.

The Nexus Point is simply the point where the business actually makes money. It is the point when you or your agent (website, salesperson, advertising etc) meets a client or customer – the ONLY person that can give you money is a client or a customer. If we divide a business up into essential categories like accounting, paperwork, team meetings, admin etc, and really put them under the microscope we will find that none of them create a nexus point opportunity. None of them create ACIP. Yeah, sure planning meetings and administration etc are all essential ingredients in a successful business but none of these endeavours create a nexus point opportunity – the opportunity to make money.

There are only two areas that create a nexus point. Sales and Marketing. These are the only areas that create ACIP, because they create and MAINTAIN a client.

'Marketing is getting them to the door,
Sales is getting them through the door.'
Brendan Nichols

Now a lot of people think that marketing is advertising. Marketing is infinitely more than advertising. Advertising is just a tiny component of the marketing mix.

Most of the marketing that people have seen is 'image' or 'institutional marketing'. However, the marketing that I have spent over 25 years researching is direct response marketing. Direct response marketing is about low cost, measurable strategies that make the cash register ring in the next few days or weeks. Image marketing is about promoting the brand of the business. Image marketing is costly, lengthy and will not necessarily make you money.

I know literally hundreds of direct response marketing techniques that are low cost and can create immediate, cash-generating results.

And yet my first experience in business seems pretty typical. Having trained tens of thousands of people on three continents and worked with countless business owners, less than 5% focused on the nexus point prior to working with me. Most are focused on do – do – work that does not create a direct profitable outcome.

One of the keys to making money therefore is to get more of your time back from unproductive areas so you can focus on the nexus point, make more money and have more time off as well!

The Seven Deadly Sins of Time

Deadly Sin of Time 1:
Not understanding the law of leverage

If you want to make more money in your business you have to understand the power of leverage. Leverage is perhaps the single biggest reason why civilisation has advanced so rapidly. For example, going back 200 years, if I wanted to personally talk to you the maximum range I could speak to you from was perhaps 50 metres – I'd have to shout but you could probably hear what I was saying. However, now I can speak to you by phone and you could be half way around the world. The phone has allowed me to leverage myself. Leverage allows you to do more with less. Electricity is nothing but a form of leverage. It allows you to do more with less – you can heat a home or use electricity to run a computer.

We can build freeways in record time because we have giant machines that can leverage the work. So the key to getting your time back so you can do more with less time is leverage.

You can either move toward your goals quickly or you can do it slowly. There is no more honour or pride in taking the long way round. In fact, taking a shortcut in any other situation is deemed sensible but in business it's assumed to be shoddy. Instead everyone thinks that the harder they work the more successful they will be.

Sorry, but that whole concept is just plain wrong. Personally I think it is a throw-back to the employee culture. As an employee it's often not about how productive you are and what you get done – you're measured by whose car is still in the car park at 8 pm. Long hours are considered a prerequisite for promotion. Whether they are working hard or playing solitaire on their computer doesn't actually seem to matter.

Whatever the reason for it – it's wrong. You have to work smarter by focusing on the right things. If I run on a trampoline for an hour that's hard work. I see so many people running on the trampoline in their business, making it much harder than it needs to be.

There is a T-shirt that I love, emblazoned on the front are the words:

'They lied; hard work has killed lots of people!'

And it's certainly killed a lot of relationships, so hard work isn't the answer either. We all have to make a contribution and do the best job we can but you don't have to extract a terrible price in order to be successful. Just get smarter about where you focus your energy and leverage that time and energy effectively.

You have to constantly be asking yourself, 'How can I

leverage this?' Look at the new technology that's available so you are always searching for ways to make money when you're not personally involved. The Internet is offering huge opportunities in that area. Constantly look for shortcuts and ways to speed up your delivery without harming your quality.

A lot of people leverage their time by hiring employees and that is one way of doing it. However, if you are not great at leading teams this can create more problems than it solves.

There is a story that I like about a union representative who visits a small factory and interviews the boss about his ten employees. The union rep wants to know what the minimum wage is of each employee, how much holiday pay they receive, superannuation payments, health plan and overtime. The boss, after going through each of his employees finally says, 'Well we have one worker who only gets paid half of what every one else gets and they work 70 hours a week instead of 40 and not only that they do not get paid any overtime or benefits.' The union rep becomes very irate and says, 'This is outrageous; take me to this person at once!' The boss stares at him and says, 'You're looking at him.'

Unfortunately, this is the fate of many owners. One way of getting around employing more people is to use a VA – virtual assistant. These are PAs who often have their own business, so you are dealing with people who have a business attitude. They can do almost everything a normal PA can do but you don't have them in your office. I have had some tremendous success using a VA. Currently I have two VAs, one of them works about 400 kilometres away and I have never met her and yet her work is first rate. You can find them by doing a search on the net – it's just a matter of interviewing them to get the right one. Here is one thing we did when searching for a VA. We asked three VAs to submit a resume. Two of them submitted a resume and one submitted a resume along with two follow-up phone calls. That's the one we picked. We then gave her a couple of small, not so important jobs to see how long it took. She delivered everything in record time and the quality was fantastic. Hire slowly is the motto – test people first.

There was a great article written in Fast Company magazine many years ago by Daniel Pink about the rise of the 'Free Agent Nation'. He has since written a book of the same title and talks about how independent workers are transforming the workplace. More and more specialists are leaving the traditional workforce to hire out their services to multiple clients. As outsourcing has become a really viable option for companies in everything from accounting to recruitment to marketing these free agents are cashing in. For the agents themselves, they gain a level of control over their working lives that has benefited them and the organisations they work for. The desire to avoid two-hour commutes and environmental concerns are also driving more and more people to work from home and offering businesses very high quality services without getting the usual headaches of employing countless staff. Finding ways to leverage your time and resources is not only sensible but a necessary step to financial wealth.

Using other people's time is just common sense. I also have a high-end credit card with a free concierge service. When

I was shopping for an expensive watch, I simply called my concierge and got them to track down the stores that sold that type of watch. If I want tickets to a show I can call them and get them to organise it – and all of this is a free service and they have always been happy to do it.

Here is something you need to remember – if you don't leverage, you work too hard!

Deadly Sin of Time 2: Email

Checking emails has become a global obsession. Everybody I talk to is checking their emails. And sure, maybe you need to do that a couple of times a day but you don't need to be online all day eagerly waiting for that little 'you've got mail' sound. It's a constant interruption because if you do keep your system open all the time you probably also drop everything as soon as you hear that little sound and go to see who has sent you a message. Even if it's just your friends sending you a stupid YouTube clip of a bulldog on a skateboard. Seriously, was that worth interrupting your day for? By the time you've left what you were doing, checked your message, watched the clip, wrote 'very funny' and sent it back and got back to your work and properly re-engaged with it – you've wasted half an hour at least!

You only need to check emails twice a day – first thing in the morning and last thing before you leave to go home. Checking email has become an addiction for so many people.

Plus it's also provided people with the perfect way to avoid confrontation. Email is a great way to hide and so people say things on email that they would never say on the phone or face-to-face. It's a great tool for business but it can also get you into a lot of trouble. I would suggest as an aside that you should never say something in email that you wouldn't say face-to-face, and when there is ever any possibility for misinterpretation don't put in an email at all – pick up the phone and sort it out properly.

The phone is an amazing way to make money and stop disagreements. Do you know you can make more money using a phone by developing personal relationships than you ever can with email? How many of you have ever thought, it's a bit messy, I don't want to deal with this, it's a bit confrontational, I don't want to make that sales call, I don't want to handle the problem – I'll just send an email. And the problem gets watered down or drags on and on.

Check your messages twice and day and get back to using the phone – ironically, it's often much quicker!

Deadly Sin of Time 3:
Mobile phones

I rarely use a mobile phone for the simple reason that I don't make any money by having one. There is no one that needs to get in touch with me that urgently that will influence whether or not my business makes money. Now that may not be the case for you but in my situation it's usually just another distraction.

If you're using it to make money then it's a great business tool that allows you to leverage your time, but if not, turn it off! We have become so dependent on mobile phones that we don't even plan our day anymore. Remember 20 years ago when you went somewhere to meet friends – you actually had to speak to them and arrange a meeting place and time. That doesn't happen anymore, instead we send SMS messages back and forth and everything is so haphazard. It doesn't save time, it wastes time. By the time you've sent six messages about your location and estimated time of arrival you could have picked up the phone and made the arrangements 20 times over.

I'm not saying that using your phone to catch up with your friends is wrong. And if you enjoy sending endless texts with some weird version of English then that's great but you have to understand how much time it's taking up. Talk to your friends when you've finished making money for the day. If your friends or family are in trouble, of course you stop everything and help, but if you're just chewing the fat over whether or not you are going out on the weekend or whether you saw the soccer last night – do it later. Unless you're waiting for a particular business call that will make you money – turn it off and get busy actually making money!

Deadly Sin of Time 4:
Not understanding that your time is limited

I know you know this but do you really understand it? You only have a limited time on this planet! Your life span will be about 4,000 weeks. That's it! That's all you've got. Look back over last week. Did you spend that precious week wisely? Did you have fun? Did you make money? Or did you find yourself 'killing time'. Who in their right mind wants to 'kill time'? It's the most precious resource you have and it's the only one that is finite so start appreciating that fact right now!

I am in a really privileged position in that I know that if I were to walk out my front door tomorrow and get run over by a bus I honestly have no regrets. The only slight regret that I would have is that I just bought two pairs of brand new skis and I haven't used them yet!

But really I could die knowing that I squeezed every last drop of enjoyment out of my life. I've travelled around the world. I've stayed in some of the most exotic hotels on the planet. I have amazing kids and a wonderful wife and I'm genuinely happy. I've had a great life. And if you don't feel that too, then you deserve to.

The game is really simple – you don't want to die with any regrets at all. Or as someone said, 'Everyone has music in them. Don't die with the music still in you'. Whatever you want to do, do it right now – begin it right now.

Deadly Sin of Time 5:
Busy time versus income time

Focusing on busy time rather than income time is also a deadly sin. There are two kinds of time. The first is busy time and that's the time you spend on things that don't make you money. The other kind of time is income time and that is, as the name would suggest, the time you spend that does have a direct effect on making money. And I'm talking specifically about business here. Spending time with my kids or going for a meal with my wife is neither income nor busy time but it's very important time to me so I'm referring to my working time only here.

In business you're either in one or the other. I'll make it really easy for you to work it out for yourself – any time you are working on your sales and marketing is income time and all the other time is busy time. The only person in the world who gives you money (apart from your dear grandmother who left you something in her will) is a client or customer and that only comes about through sales and marketing.

Deadly Sin of Time 6:
Making yourself too available

The sixth deadly sin is making yourself available to everyone all the time. You don't have to do that and often it is counterproductive for everyone. For example, if you operate an open door policy where you encourage your team to come to you if they ever want to discuss anything, that's great – but it makes people lazy!

If, on the other hand, you told your people that you were always available to discuss emergencies but for anything else you'd like to limit that access time to first thing in the morning and last thing at night you would force people to articulate their problem and try to work out their own solutions. If anyone can just come in and offload their issues they are not focused on finding solutions. If they have to wait to see you they are going to have more time to work out what's actually going on, get the facts and present a clear picture to you. In doing that, it's also highly likely that they will solve the issue themselves and not need to see you at all. Everyone is therefore much more productive.

Stop making yourself available to everyone for the slightest little thing. Empower your people to make decisions and get on with the job – that way you're really accessing the power of leverage. Not only that, but people genuinely want to feel as though they are making a difference and that their contribution is valued and important. If you are constantly available to answer every quirk or question you don't allow your people to find their own solutions and feel that sense of achievement. You are not helping yourself, or them! Give your people space to be the best they can be and let them flourish – that's the best way you can get leverage anyway. And it makes for a happier, more fulfilled, workforce.

One of the most amazing businessmen of our time has got to be Ricardo Semler. Semler is the (sort of) part-time CEO of a Brazilian company called Semco. When his father wanted him to join the family business, the usual sparks flew. Ricardo decided to move on and make his own way in the world, but his dad was keen for him to stay in the business so he handed over his shares to his 21-year-old son and went on holiday. That afternoon the new boss fired 60% of his father's senior managers and the business has never been the same. There is no permanent CEO, no rules and regulations, no HQ, no business cards, no human resources department and everyone decides who they work for and what they should be paid. Despite sounding like anarchy, the system works because he believes that people want to do a good job. He also recognises that they have lives out of work and employees are encouraged to meet their own individual goals before the corporate ones. They can come and go as they please and yet the business has grown from strength to strength and is now involved in areas it had no previous experience in. It works because if you are not good at your job you will not be chosen to be in someone's work group for the next six months. People are happy and motivated because they are free to express themselves inside and outside work and follow their instincts. Sure it doesn't always work, but what an incredible business model.

Empower your people – you'll be amazed at what happens if you do.

The main point is just stop being available all the time. This idea is also part of the reason mobile phones and email are a curse when it comes to making money. Being too available to others distracts your attention from the nexus point and that means less money in your pocket. Protect your time.

Before I leave this point I also need to remind you that this principle applies to your clients too! You've got three kinds of clients – excellent clients, average clients and poor clients. The poor clients are the ones that are always on the phone about something, they take forever to pay and then when they do it's hardly worth getting! Either move them up to average clients or fire them! Life's too short – move them on.

Instead what most business owners do is focus on their poor clients because they make the most noise and as a result they don't spend enough time and energy on their excellent clients. Apart from being unfair, it's just stupid!

Deadly Sin of Time 7:
Not applying the principal of non-engagement

Occasionally, perhaps a couple of times a year, I'll tune into talkback radio and listen to all the things that people are upset about. I do this purely for research purposes and to illustrate to myself just how powerful this last sin is.

On air I hear people ranting and raving about all sorts of things. They talk about such drivel as 'the irresponsible youth' (by the way, the older generation have been saying for centuries how youth is going to the dogs) or politics AND yet they don't DO anything about it. They just engage their mind in it. It's a guaranteed way to destroy not only your time but your levels of peace and clarity of mind. And you do need clarity of mind to make money. If your head is full of stuff, it's hard to think straight.

At the moment it's global warming. These people have obviously not mastered the principal of non-engagement. Now before you get on your high horse, I am not saying don't engage with global warming. Of course we all have to take responsibility and do everything we can about the problem. But that's my point – do everything you can and then stop thinking about it.

So many of us get upset and wound up about issues but all we ever do about it is bitch. We might not be sad enough to get on talkback radio but we bitch to our friends or our family and bore the pants off the neighbours with our constant whinging about whatever the hot topic of the day is.

What's the point – it's a complete waste of your time. So my answer is, do something about it or don't think about it. If you're upset about not making any money in your business – do something about it or stop thinking about it. If you're upset about the government – do something about it or stop thinking about it. Ideally do something about it and then stop thinking about it. But whinging won't change anything!

You only have a certain amount of attention units in your brain and if you load them up with garbage that you have no control over then there's nothing left to focus on the things you have got control over.

If you've got a problem, do something. If you're upset about the economy, do something about it. If you can't do anything about it, forget about it. If you've got a problem with the starving kids in Africa, do something about it or don't think about it. Sure you may not be able to single-handedly change poverty in Africa but as Margaret Mead once said, 'Never doubt that a small, group of thoughtful, committed citizens can change the world. Indeed, it is the only thing that ever has.' You can make a donation to a third-world charity, you could sponsor a child or sponsor a school or you could spend your holidays helping out at an orphanage in Zimbabwe. Or you could focus on making a ton of money so you can really make a financial contribution that would help change things. That's what I do. I donate money to various causes because I am concerned about the starving kids in Africa and that's doing something about it.

This isn't about being heartless, it's about head space. If something is bothering you fix it and move on. Don't let your focus and attention be robbed by something that you can't change. For example, I went into a service station recently to fill up and I used a certain credit card to pay. As soon as I put it down I could see the guy behind the counter almost recoil! He started making some comments about it and he was obviously very resentful. The card indicated a certain degree of wealth and that upset him. I could feel myself getting annoyed. But I have two options here – engage or delete. And I hit delete. In the end I chose to feel empathy for him. He was angry at me because he hated his job and I represented what he didn't think he could have. I get that, but I'm not going to waste my time stewing about it and getting upset about it.

Here is another shocker for a lot of people. I rarely read newspapers. Shock, horror and blasphemy! 'But you can't do that, you have to stay current with what's going on!' I can hear people scream. You mean I have to stay current with all the bad news? As a guy that is regarded as an expert on marketing, let me tell you a little secret. The reason that they print bad news is because that is what sells. They have tried selling 'good news' and it does not sell. So basically they scour the world for bad news and print that.

So why would I want to put that in my head every day if I

am trying to stay positive?

Here is what I do. I subscribe to some very good newsletters where I get either all the raw data, without the negative slant, and some good newsletters that provide an educated, economic picture. This, by the way, actually saves me a lot of time as well as giving me a much more accurate picture of what is going on.

Be careful what you 'engage' with. Engage with the wrong things and they will rob you of your time and energy.

GET COMPLETELY FREE

'3 Reasons People Sabotage Their Success (that very few people know about) and How to Change It'

Your mindset is vital to your success. These Powerful Secrets show you why people destroy their success. Don't fall victim to being blind-sided by a Mack truck. This mini e-book will show you how to by pass these hidden mine fields and program yourself for success. **Value $47.00**

Go now to www.RichesFromBusiness.com/FreeGift

The Four Steps to Manifesting Money into Your Life

There is a sequence to manifesting anything in your life – whether you want to make more money or anything you want to have. I remember one of the most profound moments of my life where I really witnessed this first hand.

Annie and I married only four months after we started going out. When we started seeing each other, it was nice and friendly and then after about two months it became very romantic. I asked her to dinner at the Regent Hotel, which back then was the only restaurant in Sydney that did silver service. It really was impeccable service, we were dressed to the nines and it was a wonderful evening. About three-quarters of the way through the meal a thought flashed into my mind. I'm a great believer in following your gut instinct, your intuitions, and completely out-of-the-blue came the message, 'you've got to ask her to marry you'. It was so strong and so powerful.

At first I was surprised and thought, you can just move right back out of my brain! All the logical reasons why that was a stupid idea came flooding in – apart from anything else we had only been seeing each other for a couple of months! And yet the feeling was really strong. I excused myself and went to the bathroom. I'm not kidding – I stood in front of the mirror with my hands on the wash basin, looking into my own eyes going, 'Are you crazy?' I was actually saying this out loud and thank God no one else was there! But I knew I had to act on it. I went back to sit down and Annie immediately noticed something was different too and she said, 'Why do I feel like running out of the restaurant'! I asked her to marry me and she said yes. We both lit up like a beacon and we've been together ever since.

At the time, both of us thought that it had come out-of-the-blue but it didn't, not when you consider the sequence that occurs when you translate an idea into a reality.

Our relationship started with a single isolated thought. When I first met Annie I remember thinking she seemed very interesting. I could have just left it at that and gone on with my life but I moved to step 2, where that initial thought happened more frequently. I'd find myself thinking about Annie more often. After a few weeks or a month I realised I was thinking of Annie a lot. How many people have done this when they fell in love? Pretty soon you go from a few isolated thoughts to what's called 'streaming'. And that's the point of no return – step 3. I was thinking about Annie all the time. So when we went out to dinner, manifestation was the logical next step. So it really wasn't 'out-of-the-blue' at all. And that's what you do with all the major decisions in your life.

First it starts with a single thought – perhaps you think one day that you'd like to own your own house. Pretty soon you start to think about that idea more and more. You start imagining what it would be like and what sort of furniture you would have and where you would like it to be. So the single thought gets more substance and strength. All of a sudden you're streaming – it's no longer a single isolated thought, it's something else altogether. Next thing you know you're looking at ads in the paper, you're visiting open houses at the weekend. You're visiting real estate agents in the areas that you like. Then you find one in your price range and bang! You're buying your own home.

Here are the four steps:

1. Single isolated thought

2. Multiple isolated thoughts

3. Streaming

4. Manifestation

The really big quantum leap happens when you hit step 3 and this was the stage I was at when I went out with Annie to the restaurant.

Manifesting is really fast when you're streaming. It's like that single thought opens up a door in your mind – like Alice in Wonderland – and soon it grows and grows until the door is big enough for you to walk through.

And this is how you do everything. The problem is that most people get stuck at step 1 or 2. They have the single isolated thought about how nice it would be to make more money from their business but that's about it. Or perhaps they graduate to step 2 where that thought appears every now and again but it never leaps into the streaming phase where it almost becomes an obsession.

The snap point we talked about in Chapter 2 is usually the catalyst for someone to move from step 2 to streaming and that's when things really start to change. 'Wouldn't it be nice to …' becomes, 'I've got to make more money'. A lot of the people I see in my seminars are already streaming because they are scanning the environment for anything that can get them closer to their goal. Everything about them is aligned to that vision and they are therefore pulling in the experiences, people, training and contacts that they need to make their dream a reality.

It is true that all of the major decisions in your life have followed these four steps. You fell in love this way. You bought your first house this way. You bought a car that you love this way. How many people have gone on the dream holiday after going through that process? First of all, somebody told you about Austria, for example. Wow, they've got these castles and you can drink coffee on the river and then pretty soon you're going, wow, that would be pretty cool. Then you go to step 2 and soon after that all you're thinking about is castles on the river. You're streaming.

And by the way, this is important. This is how people get into drug addictions, alcoholism. 'I'll have a drink' turns into a regular drink turns into 'I have to have a drink' and you're streaming. Unfortunately you're also an alcoholic! Same with drugs! This is the same process that people go through then they have affairs. They are in a marriage but notice someone else. Soon that's all they notice and once they are streaming it's a small step to cheating.

Steps 1 to 4 are how to create all the big positive things in your life and all the big disasters! You can stream negatively or you can stream positively. Both are equally effective in bringing about what it is you're focused on. My advice, therefore, is to be very particular about what it is that you progress into the streaming phase. Here is a classic example of how one of my clients, a young man, turned around his life by using this principle.

When he first started working with me, I was able to show him a number of direct response marketing techniques that catapulted the income of his computer repair business. Within a short time he was making a profit that varied between $18,000 a month to $22,000 a month.

However, after a year his income had radically dropped. Interviewing him I found that he was spending a lot of time with a crowd that liked to party and drink a lot. His focus had completely changed. He was no longer streaming on wealth, all his focus was now on partying. As a result a lot of the cash-generating strategies we had implemented were not being applied.

When he redirected his focus, the money started to come in once more and at the time of writing he is looking at making just over $380,000 in profit for this year.

How to Use 'The Architect' to Build Massive Motivation to Make More Money

What would happen if I put a whole lot of building equipment on a vacant block of land and asked you to build a house without a plan? It would be a complete disaster. Without detailed architects' drawings it would be a mess.

You may think this is a cliché, but seriously why should your life be any different? I am always staggered at how few people put their internal architect to work. How is it that you would think it ridiculous to attempt to build a house without a detailed plan and yet most people attempt to build a life or build a successful business without one!

Your internal architect is the part of you that develops a vision of where you want to go. When people ask me what I do, I can say something really boring like, 'I am an international speaker and a consultant'. However, that doesn't reveal what I really do. There's no plan in that description. The correct answer is, 'I take business people and put cash in their pocket.' That is my vision. I have different goals of how I do that but the VISION ALWAYS PRECEDES THE GOAL.

The most important word in the English language is 'why'. 'Why' is the reason you do everything – you ate breakfast this morning because you had a 'why' called hunger.

If you want to make a lot of money you need a strong enough 'why' to pull you through the steps so you arrive at streaming and manifest your vision. You need a why to stay motivated and the architect is the part of you that gives you that WHY.

I did a very interesting exercise in one of my seminars that really highlighted this point. David was someone who had a lot of trouble keeping his motivation. He went through peaks and troughs of performance and wanted to know what caused it. I suggested that the best way for me to explain what was happening to him was to have him demonstrate it. He agreed to do whatever I asked of him for a couple of minutes. I then got the entire seminar audience in on the act. Every time David completed a task assigned him, I asked the audience to clap and cheer like they were in a motivation seminar. I then picked up a pen and threw it about seven metres away from David. The pen hit the floor and rolled along the carpet. Looking at David I said, 'David, quick, run and get the pen!' David scooted off and immediately brought the pen straight back to me. The audience cheered and clapped at his performance.

Without giving him a chance to pause, I threw the pen

and repeated the command, 'Quick David, run and get the pen!' David took off in a sprint and once more retrieved the pen. The audience of course applauded and screamed their approval. I repeated this for several minutes. By now David was beginning to look confused. So I asked him what he was thinking. David replied, 'Well I am beginning to wonder why the hell I am doing this?' David had hit the nail on the head.

David's problem was a common one. He had set his goals and had made progress up to a certain point but he never had a strong enough 'why' once the initial motivation wore off. He didn't have a purpose that backed up his goals.

I am sure, like David, you have experienced hitting what I call the 'why brick wall'. You've been running down the road of life and all of a sudden you've asked, 'Why the hell am I doing this?' Remember that passion is motivation and motivation based on just going for a goal is short term. It's a really good bet that if your passion is waning then you may need to look at what you feel passionate about.

I was in Venice many years ago and wandered down some winding, twisting, cobblestone back alley. As I rounded the corner, there in front of me was the most exquisite café, decked out in deep mahogany timber and polished brass fittings. The waiters all wore spotless white coats and silk bow ties. I was greeted by a waiter who gave me the most extraordinary service. He treated me as if he really cared (as opposed to acting like he cared). You know I cannot remember what I ate that day, but I remember him. I believe I still have the card of that restaurant, tucked away in one of my drawers.

Everything is done there with a sense of perfection and

every guest is treated like a king or queen. It isn't an act with them, it's genuine. What makes this place so special is they have a vision to 'create an extraordinary experience'. That is the 'why' and their 'how' is by delivering, among other things, fabulous food and unforgettable service.

The trouble with goal-based motivation is that it's short lived. In the old days with my sales teams before I knew any better, I would take them to motivational seminars and they'd get really revved up. Everybody would leave feeling as though they were going to go out and make more sales and take over the world. Then I'd watch as that initial enthusiasm and passion would drain away – often leaving them feeling flatter than they had been before we went to the event!

Finally what I came to realise is that the fundamental driving force of passion, and hence motivation, is PURPOSE. You've got to have a purpose.

If you don't, you will constantly feel these highs and lows of motivation! If you have a purpose, on the other hand, you have a big enough 'why' to sustain you through those natural ups and downs. You are able to bring everything you do back to some simple home truths about who you are and what you want to do in your life. Having a powerful purpose is the hallmark of excellence in any field.

Think of it like this. When some of the indigenous tribes would go walking for long distances they would assign one person to be the keeper of the flame. As you can imagine there were times when it was very difficult to make a fire. So the person who was assigned this role would take a smouldering piece of coal, or something that kept the flame alive, and their sole job was to keep the flame burning. Perhaps it would be better described as their soul job! When you discover your purpose or assign yourself a purpose you are keeping the fire alive in your soul. When our flame goes out, we are in big trouble because then we don't know why we are doing what we are doing and we lose our way and our motivation. But with a strong-enough why and a powerful-enough purpose, we can always navigate ourselves back on track.

Often the big focus in seminars is setting goals. And sure you do have to know what it is you're trying to achieve, and goals are important, but goals are always secondary to purpose.

Goals without purpose are as potent as the average New Year's Resolution! And we all know how many of them come to fruition.

Your internal architect directs your life in accordance with your innate drive or abilities. It is what determines your purpose. There has been a lot said about purpose as though we each have some very specific reason for being alive. We are encouraged to find our purpose and then miraculously all of life will fall neatly into place. I'm not saying that. I don't believe it's that simple and it's certainly not that neat. You can just as easily decide what your purpose is as you can discover it. Often people will find a purpose when there are people involved that they love deeply. Someone will commit to their business and making more money because they have a family and that family gives their life a purpose. The most powerful purpose always seems to involve helping other people. Human nature dictates that we will always do more for those we care about than we will do for ourselves. Finding a purpose that makes other people's lives easier, better, happier in some way is a strong motivating force. When there is a deeper meaning to your actions, that well-spring of motivation can be tapped whenever you feel jaded by your goals.

There are always going to be ups and downs in your life. If there wasn't, you'd be dead! Having a purpose or a grand vision, however, makes the navigation of those ups and downs easier. Without that you may find yourself in a low and not have the motivation or the pull to move you through it.

As Victor Frankl, author on Man's Search for Meaning and survivor of the Nazi concentration camps said, 'A man who becomes conscious of the responsibility he bears toward a human being who affectionately waits for him, or to an unfinished work, will never be able to throw away his life. He knows the "why" for his existence, and will be able to bear almost any "how".'

If you're unsure what your purpose is you will find the 12 drivers from Chapter 7 useful to review. Remember you ranked them in order of importance. The first three will probably hold a clue to what your 'why' is.

Say, for example, that you discovered that your key drivers were pursuit of excellence and creativity, you wouldn't be surprised to realise that these aspects of your make-up figured in your purpose. In my case, contribution is important and creativity also plays a part in that. My purpose encapsulates those things because I am still able to play around with creative ideas about how to ensure my clients make the most money from their business and I am able to feel a genuine sense of contentment because I know that what I do meets my purpose of putting money in business owners' pockets. The particular strategies and how I do that is where I am able to express my creative side. Even though I have learned that I must temper that creativity with commercial viability sometimes.

So if you're unsure of your purpose go back to Chapter 7 and see what you ranked in your top 3 or 4. Look back in your life and highlight five or six times where you have felt great about what you were doing. Perhaps you completed a certain project. Try and identify a few pivotal moments and re-assess them from the perspective of your top drivers. You may be surprised to see a correlation. Perhaps you will see for the first time that all of the really great experiences of your life have been when you have felt truly recognised. Or perhaps you identify that it doesn't actually matter if anyone else knew what you did. Perhaps you can see that the experience helped others in some way and you felt that your contribution was valid. Perhaps you were in a flow state as you struggled with a challenge, only to find a creative and powerful solution.

These glimpses into your previous successes can help you to clarify your purpose. The architect is your vision of what you are about. Once you know that, you just have to find the right vehicle that allows you to live that vision.

GET COMPLETELY FREE

'Create a Stampede of New Business and Profits'

The 10 rules of the successful entrepreneur. A powerful 10 day course on discovering the tools to turn yourself into a highly successful entrepreneur.

Go now to www.RichesFromBusiness.com/FreeGift

Making Money a Priority – Setting Goals and Aligning Them to Your Vision

Establishing what your vision is for your life will enable your inner architect to create accurate plans for its creation. Part of that process, of course, is the individual goals within that vision. Like the restaurant I mentioned in the previous chapter, their vision was to create an extraordinary experience but the individual goals that went into making that a reality were constantly evolving. Their focus on the food quality probably involved a myriad of smaller goals, including sourcing the very best ingredients, quality of staff, cleanliness of the kitchen etc. The service probably also involved many individual goals including training, length of shifts etc.

You may have seen this a thousand times before and chances are that familiarity with the subject has given you valid reason to dismiss it. Don't! Every single one of my clients who is a millionaire sets goals. It is absolutely crucial to your success.

Apart from anything else if you don't get really clear about what it is you're trying to achieve you won't activate your RAS, your internal radar system. Remember we talked about this part of your brain in Chapter 4. Unless you are consciously aware of what it is you're aiming for, then your internal filter system may delete relevant information and you might miss opportunities to make your goals a reality.

So do it right now ... Grab some paper and a pen or open a new document on your computer. Do NOT read this as an academic exercise. You need to get involved – it could be the most powerful thing you do this year!

Step 1

Choose three goals for your business and two goals for your personal life. If you set too many you can split your focus and can lead to self-sabotage. It's easy to focus on a few things but too many may water everything down. It's important to include a balance of professional and personal goals because life is a balance of both and so that should be reflected in your goals. Otherwise you may find that your business is booming but you have no friends or loved ones to enjoy your success with. I can't imagine that would be that much fun!

Choose some goals that will excite you and get you to stretch outside your comfort zone. The key is to stretch yourself - not break yourself. Which leads us to point 2.

Step 2

Choose only goals that you are passionate about. Don't add in goals because they look good if someone happens to find them! If you don't genuinely have the passion for something, don't put it on the list – it won't happen. So that means that while you're aiming for three professional goals and two personal – if you only have two professional and one personal goal that you're passionate about then stick to them.

You also need to make sure your professional and personal goals don't conflict. Let's say that your business goals are to make $250,000 in net profit, double your staff and increase the number of hours you work in your business. Then let's say that your personal goals were to spend more time with your family and take more holidays. If your personal goals are more passionate than your business goals then that is probably what will happen and vice versa. Plus, if you want to double the time you work in your business, how can you spend more time with your family?

Step 3

Write your chosen goals down, along with the reason you want them to happen. This is where your goals need to align with your purpose. If they don't they just won't happen. The most powerful word in the English language is 'why'. If you want to make a million dollars, you have to have a very powerful 'why'. We all know the story of poor immigrants who became multi-millionaires. They had a very powerful 'why'.

Step 4

Look at your list and determine the goals you are most passionate about. Then place them in the order that is most important to you.

Step 5

Assess each goal using the MAST formula.

M stands for measurable

Too often, people set unquantifiable goals and as a result they are meaningless and hold no power. Part of the reason is because someone may not want to appear 'greedy' or doesn't want to be disappointed so they might specify that they want to 'make more money'. Making $2 is making more money but would you be pumped to make an extra $2? 'Making more money' doesn't mean much because it's not precise enough. Make your goals quantifiable so that you can measure whether or not you meet them. So instead of saying 'make more money', you might specify that you will 'make an extra $100,000 net profit from your business in the first six months of the year' – that's measurable and therefore it becomes a real target.

In six months you will know whether or not you've met that goal.

A stands for achievable

Your goal needs to be achievable. So, for example, if you set a goal of becoming a billionaire within the next two years but the most you have ever made is $80,000 a year – that's probably not achievable! It's pie-in-the-sky dreaming and that's not helpful to anyone. An achievable goal may be to 'make $500,000 in the next three years'. That's definitely a stretch from the position you are now at but it's a realistic stretch. You have to choose a goal that you believe is achievable, considering your starting point. Choosing goals that are not achievable is a self-sabotage pattern I see all the time. The ego gets in the way and people put in these lofty aspirations that have no way of becoming reality. And deep down they know it!

They are setting up the failure because they haven't even begun the journey toward the goal. By aiming for a target they can't possibly hit, they get the 'perfect excuse' for failure right at the start. 'Yeah, but I was really going for the big one'. These are the people that want to go from zero to hero overnight and have all the excuses ready when it doesn't happen.

Remember the key is to stretch yourself, not break yourself.

S stands for specific

Making your goals as specific as possible focuses your attention and makes the pleasure of achievement all the sweeter. Often people are afraid to get too specific because a) they don't actually know what they want and b) it feels limiting in some way. Nothing could be further from the truth – making your target very specific brings it to life. The more description you provide about your ideal scenario, the more feeling and passion you can create for attainment.

What feels better, 'I want to make more money so I can buy a nice car' or 'I will make an additional $100,000 net profit from my business in the first six months of this year? As my reward I will buy a black Porsche 911 with leather seats and drive down the Ocean Road with my partner to celebrate!'

Being specific about your goals gives them juice that can be drawn upon when you need to re-engage with your vision and push past the obstacles that you WILL meet.

So make it very clear and specific and write it down. To quote Mark Victor Hansen – 'don't think it, ink it.'

T stands for time

Put a specific time on when you want to complete your goal otherwise you could find you are chasing it forever!

In the example above, if I didn't specify when I wanted to

make that additional $100,000 then I won't know whether I've achieved it or not.

If I said to you that I wanted to get $10 in ten minutes then that fits the MAST formula. However, it is not very inspiring. Your goals should stretch you and inspire you. Stretch is the key word here. You want to stretch but not break – that is why we choose goals that are achievable. And if you get into the habit of setting goals in six-month intervals then the stretch that you will achieve over a ten-year period can be phenomenal.

Step 6

Give your goals emotional momentum. We create things that have emotional meaning to us and without that emotional element your goal isn't going to happen. We are emotionally-driven creatures – all great salespeople know this. We buy with our heart and justify the purchase later using our head.

If you create your goals from your head you're going to struggle to find and keep the emotional intensity required to sustain you during difficult times. So you need to add emotion and the way to do that is to vividly imagine what your life would be like if you were to achieve that goal. Imagine what it would be like to drive down the Ocean Road in a brand new Porsche … You need to really engage your creative powers and feel how great it would feel.

But there is another element to this that is often overlooked in goal-setting instructions. First, you have to vividly imagine what your life would be like if you did not achieve that goal. Imagine the disappointment, imagine what your friends and family would say if after all your posturing you didn't do a damn thing? Imagine how hard it would be financially; imagine how your kids would feel when you were not able to get them the things they really wanted. Get really clear that you don't want to experience that and then imagine how you would feel if you did meet your goals.

The twin forces of feeling what you don't want and feeling what you do want will create emotional momentum. This is a very powerful way of increasing your passion toward your goals and vision.

Step 7

Be grateful for what you already have around you. I have noticed in the past that the more I am grateful for what I already have, the more seems to have come my way. There is another reason for this. Having examined countless successful people, the vast majority of these people share a common trait. They are upbeat and optimistic. Optimism is a powerful 'success attractor'. Gratitude is one of the best ways to increase your optimism level.

FA$T

FA$T

Financial Acceleration $uccess Techniques (FA$T) – Low cost powerful techniques to increase your income

We've talked a lot in this book about the structure of wealth – having the right mindset and changing your perspective on how you run your business. Now it's time to get down to the nitty gritty of what you need to do to put more cash in your pocket.

There are only five ways to generate cash in your business. I've been offering a reward in my seminars for years to anyone who can come up with a sixth but no one has claimed the reward. Why? Because there isn't a sixth!

There are five ways to increase business cash:

1.   Increase the number of clients.

2.   Increase the amount of purchases from customers

or clients that you already have. This philosophy is called maximisation. Maximisation is an art that can be condensed into literally hundreds of specific principles. I cover more of these principles in my seminars and audio programs. However, the ones contained in this book will be enough to get you started.

3.   Increase your prices – how much you charge.

4.   Cut expenses or overheads.

5.   Develop a business that is a saleable asset. In other words, selling the business for a big profit.

The next **21** chapters of this book are all 'must do' Financial Acceleration $uccess Techniques. If you are serious about making more money in your business then these are the fastest routes possible to accelerated wealth and success. There are no extra points to doing it slow. You can climb a mountain or take a helicopter, that is the FA$T track!

They are presented in bite-sized sections so that you only get the information you need. I'm not here to blind you with science of marketing theory, just solid predictable techniques for increasing revenue. And because they are broken up into manageable bite-sized sections you can simply commit to implementing one at a time. But buckle up – you're about to discover how to make more money – FA$T!

Please understand these are not academic theories. They

have all been tested in the real world. Many of my clients have doubled their income (and more) by using these FA$T principles. I have seen people who have struggled for years make astounding jumps in their success simply by using these proven formulas.

Free Up Some Time and Discover How To Work Less!

This first step and the first FA$T is incredibly important. The simple fact is that if you don't free up some time it doesn't matter what the remaining techniques tell you because you won't do any of them.

And instead of fast-tracking your journey to wealth all I'll succeed in doing is fast-tracking your journey to despondency. All you're going to get is a renewed sense of failure as you add even MORE things to your 'to do' list that you know will never get done! And that's not going to help anyone!

If you are already a business owner, I have little doubt that you are already stretched to breaking point. I know that you are the proverbial duck on water – calm on the outside and paddling like a banshee underneath. Or perhaps you've dispensed with the formalities and are paddling like a banshee on the outside too! Everyone, including you, knows you are drowning, so the idea of changing things or adding things is just too much to bear so you will ignore the advice and struggle on as before. And I really don't want you to do that because I know that what is contained in these 21 chapters could revolutionise your business. No hype, just things that really work in the real world.

So the only way that you will even try this stuff is if you can recover some time to dedicate to it. And that's why this step, while not very exciting, is imperative to your success. You have to find some time to implement the rest.

Consider all the variables of being human – there are thousands, and yet we all have red blood running through our veins, we all need oxygen and water and we all have 24 hours in our days. We still need to eat and we still need to sleep and I'm certainly not advocating that we cut into time spent with loved ones, so we need to be clever in finding it from somewhere else!

Remember in Chapter 13 we talked about the seven deadly sins of time and the distinction regarding the nexus point, and busy time versus income time. If you don't remember, go back and re-read the chapter. You have to understand this. In my seminars when I go through this process I always explain the difference of busy time (tasks that do not directly produce ACIP – actual cash in pocket) and income time (ACIP tasks) and then get each person to review how much of their day is spent in which area. There is always this strange silence that comes over the room as the penny drops. After all, it's common sense. When you know the nexus point, the point where the customer or prospective customer meets your business in a sales situation – be that through salespeople, advertising, your website or other direct response marketing techniques – then it makes sense that the only time you will make money is when you are spending time working on aspects of that nexus point. Essentially, you only make money when you are engaged in income time.

Everything else is busy time.

Every time I ask people to apportion their week based on these two types of work almost everyone in the room realises that they spend about 90% of their time in busy time. You don't make money in busy time. You might be doing things that are important and necessary for your business but you don't make money. As Goethe reminds us, 'Things that matter most, should never be at the mercy of things that matter least.'

So the first thing you need to do is highlight for yourself how much time you spend on busy time versus income time so you can recover some time.

Write down all the activities you currently do under both categories then calculate the percentage of time you spend in 'busy time' and 'income time'.

The things I do in 'busy time' are:

....

....

....

....

....

....

....

....

....

....

The percentage of time I spend in 'busy time' is
.....................%

The things I do in 'income time' are:

....

....

....

....

....

....

....

....

....

....

The percentage of time I spend in 'income time' is
.....................%

Finding more time means learning to:

a)   Delegate busy time tasks to harness the power of
       leverage

b)   Delay busy time tasks

c)   Stop checking your email every five minutes

d)   Turn your mobile phone off

e)   Limit your availability

f)   Practise non-engagement – if something's on your
       mind, do something about it or forget it

**Word of warning – Don't fall into the delegation deception
trap**

Delegating tasks is, in theory, a great way to free up your
time. It allows you to leverage your available resources and
get on with doing what only you as the manager or leader
can do. The trouble is delegation can be a hotbed of personal
deceptions. While the theory is sound the reality turns out
to be nothing more than a string of 'valid' ways for you to
avoiding actually delegating.

Deception 1

The first deception is when you think that unless you do a task yourself you won't get the credit. Unless you do it all you will actually miss out on the accolades. This is a very narrow perspective and assumes that physical work is as useful and valuable as strategy and planning. Both are necessary parts of success but you as the leader need to focus on income time – whatever that may be.

Deception 2

The second deception is when you avoid delegating because you just want to be liked by everybody and asking others to do unpopular tasks will not always win you new friends. But your job as owner and leader of your business is not necessarily to win friends, your job is to win sales and create a strong vibrant business that actually makes you money.

Deception 3

The third delegation deception can be summed up by the phrase, 'If you want something done right, do it yourself.' The reason you don't delegate is because you have no faith in your peers or your staff. Instead, often with an air of irritating superiority, you decide to do everything yourself and lament how you just can't get the staff these days.

But seriously is that really true? If it is then it perhaps says more about your own inadequacies as a trainer rather than any deficiency in other people. If it is true, then you need to sort out your staffing issues and find people who are capable of taking instruction and who have initiative. Stop bitching about it and get good people. Plus, by constantly undermining your faith in others and assuming their incompetence before ever giving them a fair trial, you are actually preventing your people from growing and learning. It really is amazing just how capable people become when they are trusted to be so. You have to give people the chance and accept that everyone makes mistakes when learning a new skill.

You have to get into the habit of expecting the best from others, train them well and give them the encouragement they need to rise to the challenge. That means you have to be mindful of who you delegate to. Choosing the wrong person is not the other person's fault – you have to be careful who you choose.

Deception 4

The fourth delegation deception is when you avoid asking others to share the load as a way of maintaining power. If you keep control of that task you will protect your 'trade secrets' or specialist knowledge and that way you get to feel more important than you would otherwise. Again this is short-sighted – the more people that can do your daily tasks the better. And this goes for everyone in the business, allowing one person to build up expertise and knowledge without ever getting that down into systems and processes means you can very often be held to ransom by that person. The more competent people you have in your business who can adequately cover for others, the better your business will be.

Deception 5

The fifth delegation deception is for those that just don't have the time to delegate. Rather than just take a little time to explain what you need and communicate your expectations, it's supposedly easier just to do it yourself. Sure it might be once, but it certainly isn't when you are doing that task time and time again. Again it's a lazy and shortsighted way to run your business. Yes, I said lazy ... Sure it can be easier to do something yourself but easy isn't always better. Involving others and communicating what you need does take a little more time but it's time well spent. You can't do everything, so the sooner you let go and start using delegation to help develop your team and your business the quicker you're going to get rich.

As a business owner and leader you have to learn to delegate effectively.

Lock Tight Systems to Decrease Your Workload

Okay, this one can make your life easier and if you do it right can actually make you money while you sleep (I do this in a number of ways, one of which is Internet marketing). Creating systems for your business is one of the only techniques that will make you money in a variety of ways. Remember there are only five ways to make money – sell to more people, sell more often, increase the price, reduce your costs, or create a saleable asset.

Systemising your crucial business processes hits the mark on four out of those five methods – now that is leverage. If you systemise your business, you don't have to keep reinventing the wheel so you reduce costs, you can fine-tune your selling process and deliver a more consistent performance and that helps to increase sales and repeat business. Plus if you are serious about creating a saleable asset then your prospective buyer wants to know that they will be able to replicate your success and that means systems.

The irony of systems is that people think that they are restricting and boring. The truth is they are totally liberating. You don't get bound up in wondering if you're doing things right, new staff get up to speed much faster and everyone knows exactly what's expected of them. That's liberating. You don't have to channel all your creativity into spinning plates; instead you can focus that creative energy elsewhere and really make the business buzz.

One of the greatest business leaders of all time, Tom Watson at IBM, said this, 'Everyday at IBM was a day devoted to business development, not doing business. We didn't do business at IBM, we built one.' And Tom Watson was one of the first people to coin this phrase, 'working in a business as opposed to working on a business'.

People that work in a business usually have no systems, people that work on a business are constantly refining their business as a structure. They are refining that structure and creating a system that will work for everybody in the organisation, and more importantly, building it into a saleable asset.

Henry Ford was one of the first people to really capitalise on systems. He took what was, at the time, a high-end luxury product and created it on a production line. This meant that he could deliver a consistent end-product – Ford reportedly said, 'you can have any colour Model T Ford you want as long as it's black'. Each worker would be in charge of a specialist function in a certain area, rather than one person doing the entire job. Somebody would do the wheels, somebody would drop in the engine, somebody would screw in the nuts, and it would all work on a production line all in one sequence. Because of this system, his implementation of systemised production lines brought the cost of producing a car down and he revolutionised the automotive industry. For the first time a car came within the financial reach of the masses and Henry Ford became extremely wealthy as a result.

You need to think like Henry Ford and systemise your business. You need to take the chance out of the process of product, or service quality, and delivery, and you need to elevate the customer's experience to one that automatically results in repeat sales. Yes, there is an investment of time required to pull this off but it is essential if you are serious about making serious money from your business.

Let's look at the keys to creating a really great system

Step 1

You have to develop a system that can be operated by people of any kind of skill level. If it's a system that only two other people on the planet can operate, then it really isn't an effective system, because it requires a high level of skill.

Step 2

You've got to clearly document the systems. It's got to be written down; otherwise, again, it's just locking up the system inside somebody's head. If how something is done is in someone's head, not on paper, then it makes you and your business 'people-dependent' rather than 'systems-dependent.' What happens when that person leaves the company, or worse, they have an accident or are off ill for months? Your business suffers – so get the knowledge down on paper. Create a system that is clearly documented.

Step 3

Make sure that your systems create more order, rather than less order. A system needs to be a consistent shortcut to an outcome. So don't over complicate the system and make it as effective and streamlined as possible.

Step 4

The system has got to produce a clearly-defined outcome. If the system, for example, creates a model T motorcar every time, then it is a system. But if we've got a system that creates marshmallows one day and teaspoons the next, that's not a system, that's an ad hoc procedure. Answering the phone is just an outcome until you create a system around it that specifies how you answer the phone. If the system specifies that you must answer the phone within three rings and answer with a specific greeting then it becomes a system. If you know the procedure to follow should the person the caller wishes to speak to not be available, then that's a system. If the fact that caller must be called back within 24 hours is written into the procedure, then it's a system. If you tell your new receptionist 'You've got to answer the phone' then how and when he or she does that is open to interpretation. And that is rarely a good thing!

Increase the Number of Clients to Make More Income

This is obvious right? Well, yes it is and yet it's amazing how little time business owners spend thinking about it. All too often they are so busy paddling to stand still with the customers they have that the idea of more isn't actually that appealing! And that's why locking down your systems is so important. You have to get the systems in place so that new customers can come into the business without diminishing the level of care shown to the ones you already have! If that happens it won't matter if you find new clients, their experience will be so bad they won't come back, so all your effort will have been for nothing.

If, on the other hand, you get your systems locked down so there is a consistency in the quality of product or service delivery then you are in a position to increase your customer base and keep them.

Every business starts with a few customers so the reach is small. In order to make more money you have to increase that reach out into other sectors so that your potential customer base is constantly expanding. The bottom line is that if you have no new clients or you are losing clients faster than you are finding them then your revenue will dry up. Now, I'm going to let you into a little secret. It's really quite obvious but comes as a revelation to so many. Here's the secret –

'No clients, No cash.'

The reality for business owners of all sizes, especially young businesses, is that their business-generation techniques are limited to one or two. Say you have a family-run bakery. The only business generation method you have is walk-in traffic. That's the only way you get business, consequently you're operating with a limited audience and it's really hard work! Your business is doing okay but you're tired. Your whole life revolves around your one shop – serving customers, buying supplies, preparing food etc! You get home one night and you've reached your snap point.

You really need to increase your customer numbers so your time spent in the store is worthwhile! So you put an ad in the paper advertising 'Free muffin with a cup of the best coffee in town on Tuesdays', because you've realised Tuesdays are a particularly slow day. Now you've got more clients coming in and you realise for every five new customers, two become regulars for the rest of the week as well. Now you've added another stream to your business.

Truth is there are very, very few businesses that have more

than two business-generation methods. Most will rely on walk-past traffic and a little advertising. That's it.

Some businesses might use advertising. Another business might use direct mail. Another business might use telemarketing. Another business might use a sales force, actually in the field door-knocking, but very few businesses employ any more than two of the dozens of methods available. And yet you need to increase the ways you reach the customer if you are ever going to increase your customer base long term.

Think of your business – how many ways of reaching or communicating with clients and potential clients do you have?

Ways to contact your potential customers:

- Walk-in traffic
- Direct mail
- Advertising
- Household drops
- Editorial in local newspaper
- Publicity
- Internet
- E-zines by email
- Newsletter
- Sponsorship of local events
- Events
- Telemarketing

- Salesforce
- Referrals

Write down how many business generation methods you currently employ.

Stretch your mind for this one:
What other business generation methods could you add?

Find the Right Kind of Clients

Chapter 13 talked about protecting yourself from bad clients because they were thieves of your time. So before we go rushing off to put more runs on the board, let's take a minute to work out what kind! You have three types of clients. The first client is excellent and will probably account for 20% of your client base and 80% of your profit. They're the ones that you need to focus on cloning and rewarding!

If you've got a coffee shop, they're the ones you give a free coffee to every now and again. These are the ones you thank and remind of your best deals and offer extra discounts to.

This doesn't often happen, partly because business owners can be too tight and partly if the owner is not on the front line they may not have empowered their staff to be able to take that initiative. These clients are the cream of your crop and you need to treat them accordingly. Remember it's the little things that make all the difference.

There's a little coffee shop in my area and the owner has got a special meal that he only makes for me. Do I keep going back? You better believe I do – because he makes a great stir fry – but perhaps more importantly because he makes me feel good! Now I just have to walk in there and he says, 'Brendan, would you like your special?' Now when someone says, 'Would you like your special?', how does that make you feel? How many people like to feel special? Everyone! Your job is to either reward your best clients financially through discounts, or give, a more powerful reward by doing something special that they appreciate. Oh, and don't assume they will work it out. Make sure you tell them what you've done. That might sound contrived but if you don't let them know, they can either miss what you've done or assume it's all part of the service and the benefit is lost. Plus they don't get to feel special if they miss it, so it's win/win all around.

The second client is the average client. These clients are okay, there are not a lot of problems, but you know you are not getting a lot of mileage with them. When you have an average client your job is to turn them into an excellent client. Try to move people up the ladder.

The third kind of client is a pain in the neck. You know the ones I'm talking about … If you can't move these guys up the ladder to average or excellent then you need to let them go so they can become your competitor's headache! These people take too much time and life is too short to put up with unnecessary headaches.

Do you know which is which?

A great way to analyse your customers is to work out their lifetime value. How long do your customers stick around? Most people have no idea how long a customer stays with their business on average. Yet it's a very important point.

What happened to them? Where did they go? Did you upset them or did they just forget about you? You might be surprised to know that in retail and many service industries you will lose 8% of your customer base every month if you don't contact them.

All my clients will tell you they get a regular contact mostly through email, often with great value-added information at least every three weeks. Usually people stop buying because someone else has got on their radar ahead of you.

Even if you're not always selling something you need to keep in regular contact with your customer base – just to remind them you're still there and want to help them.

It's not a difficult equation – if you can sell a little more to those people you have and keep doing so for a little longer then you'll make more money. If you can do that while expanding your client base then you'll make even more money.

What is the approximate lifetime value of your average customer right now?
This can be calculated by multiplying what the average client spends with you each year by the average length of time a client stays with you.

How can I add value to my best clients so as to increase their lifetime value?
*Imagine what would happen to your business if you could increase the lifetime value of just 20% of your clients from one year to three! And these clients don't cost you anything to procure – you already have them!

Devise a strategy on what you are going to do with each of your three types of clients.

The Secret of the 'Starving Crowd' – How to Find Amazing Products That Are Easy to Sell

If I had a dollar for every time someone had told me about their latest great idea for their business, I'd be able to eradicate third world debt! And it never ceases to amaze me just how myopic people can be when it comes to their great ideas! Just watch an episode or two of 'Dragon's Den' on TV.

I remember hearing about one episode in the UK where someone pitched for an investment in an animation kit. You could put this unit on like a backpack and move around out of sight and an animated character would appear on a screen, which would do whatever you did and spoke what you spoke in an animated voice! There was no question that the gadget was clever, but who on earth would use it? What possible application does it have?

It was a classic example of one of the biggest mistakes business owners or would-be business owners make … Getting passionate about a product without any investigation into whether or not there is a market for it.

Legendary copywriter Gary Halbert tells a simple story that has a profound message. He once asked a crowd in one of his seminars what they thought they would need in order to create a successful food stand. The audience shouted out various responses, 'Great location', 'Good quality food', 'The right sauces', 'You would need to do a leaflet drop', 'You'd have to look good and have a uniform', 'You'd have to create strategic alliances'. The list was endless and after about ten minutes Halbert stopped them and said, 'No what you really need to have for a successful food stand is a starving crowd.'

I've seen it time and again where business owners decide that the world needs their product but the reality is there is no starving crowd for that business. Sure all the other things about the food stand were important, and would certainly make a good food stand a great food stand, but unless there was a starving crowd none of it would matter!

So do you have a starving crowd?

You may be reading this thinking I don't have a starving crowd! What I produce or offer isn't really something that people are desperate for. Don't be so sure.

Having presented business seminars around the world, one of the most frequent statements I hear from people struggling is, 'I am waiting for the right idea. I know when I find it, I can make a killing.' If they don't say it like that, then it is words to that effect.

The most successful people in the world do not have that kind of thinking – they take existing ideas and tweak them. They improve an existing concept.

If you can burn those words into your brain it may save you a lot of heartache. Now it does occasionally happen that someone invents something that has never been done before and makes millions. However, it is not the norm. Trying to do this would be like sitting around waiting for your numbers to come up in the lottery – it might happen but it's rare.

Let me give you some examples of what successful people do.

Henry Ford did not invent the car, but he was the first to create an assembly line. He created the model T Ford. He took an existing concept and improved upon it.

Harry Potter was not the first book ever written about boyhood adventure and magic. Books like this have been around a long time. However JK Rowling just improved on an existing concept.

What you want to do is look at existing concepts and see how you can improve upon them. This is infinitely easier than trying to invent the wheel. It is much better to improve the wheel. The wheel has been invented already – it is thousands of years old. If you look at wheels over time you will notice a continued level of improvement over those thousands of years. A modern tyre makes a wheel infinitely more functional and each stage of its evolution has made someone else rich.

The other point about finding good ideas is that it doesn't matter what you think – it is what the market thinks.

Let me give you an example. In the area where I live there was a very smart young guy who owned a café and ran it with the help of one assistant chef. The décor and atmosphere was 'relaxed, modern beachside'. It fitted perfectly into the beachside surroundings. The locals loved it because it was exactly the sort of thing they wanted. Our clever café owner simply gave the market what they wanted. He built it up to its peak and then sold it.

The new owners, however, had other ideas of what THEY wanted (yes, I did put that in capitals for a reason). They had no experience of marketing or business and had never run a restaurant. However, they spent an absolute fortune doing the café up in a modern, inner city style.

They changed the menu and doubled the staff, putting them all in identical black uniforms. All because they liked inner city style and thought the uniforms looked sophisticated. They were very nice people, they meant well but they got burnt because people simply stopped coming. If relaxed beach goers wanted inner city cool they would have gone to the inner city! They made the cardinal sin of doing what they liked and stopped listening to what the market liked.

Now compare this with Sir Richard Branson. He took an existing concept – an airline – and improved on it. He is also known to often travel on his planes and walk down the aisles asking the passengers what they like and don't like. He listens to the market.

If you asked me, 'Brendan would you prefer to take an average product with great marketing or a great product with poor marketing?', then I would probably choose the product with great marketing. There is a saying, 'Build a better mousetrap and the world will beat a path to your door'. It's a nice saying but it's just not true. It doesn't actually matter if you build the best product in the world, if people don't know about it, it's irrelevant. Microsoft wasn't necessarily the best product at the time but it had the best marketing.

In our busy modern world there is simply too much noise. Too many ads, too many distractions. So unless your mousetrap can break through that noise it will probably gather dust.

The big clue is marketing. Which leads me to our next point … What is a great product or service? A great product or service is one which people desperately need. Notice I said need. Not what you think they need. It is much easier to feed a starving crowd than people who are not hungry. You might think they need it, but you need to find out if they really do through great research.

The key is good market research. If you absolutely know you can get the clients or customers then you are a long way ahead of the game.

Who could YOUR starving crowd be?

FA$T 6

Expand Your Thinking So You Can Spot Amazing Opportunities for Greater Financial Success

A friend of mine who was a champion ice skater told me a very interesting story. She said that when she skated on a crowded ice rink she never saw the people, she saw the gaps in between the people.

It made me think. The few times I have skated I was hopeless at it. I always saw all the obstacles whereas she saw all the opportunities.

In the business arena you need to see the gaps that other people do not see. For example, most business owners (or people in general) are just busy trying to get through their 'to do list'.

Their focus is like the amateur skater who is concentrating on the people rather than the gaps. Start by asking the question, 'What do I want to achieve?' For example, my ice

204

skating friend wanted to find a clear course to where she wanted to go.

Expand your thinking around that idea so that you can identify the gaps. Fortunes have been made by people that could see the gaps! One of my favourite stories is of Cheung Yan, the founder of Nine Dragons, China's largest provider of container cardboard.

I have to agree it's not sexy, but Cheung Yan is the richest self-made woman in the world – that means richer than JK Rowling and ever richer than the billionaire Oprah Winfrey. So how did she do it? She was made redundant and with her redundancy payout she decided to plug a gap in the market. She had been trading paper as part of her previous job and put two and two together and made billions.

China was, and still is, in a growth phase, making everything from microwaves to toys to white goods. All of those products have one thing in common – they all need a cardboard box. There are not enough trees in China to sustain all the products that need a box.

Cheung Yan looked to America. In America they had a different problem – too much waste paper. So Cheung Yan bought the waste at a knock-down price, she then shipped that paper back to recycling plants in China and made cardboard boxes out of it to supply the hungry Chinese consumable market. Those goods were then shipped back to America and sold and so the cycle began again.

At every stage of the process she made money. She spotted two gaps – a problem in the US and an opposite problem in China and made money solving both. And she is helping the environment in the process as the same resource is recycled indefinitely. It's brilliant – in fact, it's so brilliant you wonder why no one thought of it before. Chances are they did, but Cheung Yan got off her chair, took a risk with her limited redundancy money and became richer than most people's wildest dreams.

Don't think like everyone else!

Giorgio Armani, a billionaire who is 72, says he likes to hang out with people who are much younger than himself because it stimulates new ideas and creativity.

One of the best ways to come up with great ideas is to start an 'entrepreneurs club' with like-minded, creative people and then brainstorm.

I have a friend whom I occasionally visit, who is totally 'off the wall'. A lot of his ideas are bordering on ridiculous but every now and again he comes up with something brilliant.

They say the line between madness and genius is very fine and I think that's very true.

Do not isolate yourself from these lateral-thinking geniuses. And remember, if you come up with something out of the box, expect resistance from the mainstream. Even his close friends, including Bob Hope, thought Walt Disney's idea of Disneyland was ridiculous and would never take off.

Read inspirational books

Read the works of those who are successful. Being able to tap into the mind of other creative people can stimulate you and inspire you to greatness.

Here is a huge tip – the greatest ideas and the most amazing opportunities will come when you are inspired! Keep the fires of your inspiration burning!

The vast majority of people are not inspired because they do not have inspiring dreams or visions (which brings me back to where we started). Get a dream that turns you on!

And remember, if you are overworked and burnt out, then it's very hard to be inspired.

Some of my greatest ideas have come when I am in inspirational places – like the ocean, the mountains or beautiful parts of Europe. Take the time to vacation in amazing places, spend time in nature and do what renews and inspires you.

How a Simple USD (that less than 1% of people use) Can Radically Increase Your Profits!

This strategy is incredibly powerful. One of my clients was Les Seabright who had a tiny part-time business in the craft industry. Being a mum she could only afford to spend minimal time per week on her business. She came to one of my seminars and then joined my coaching group where we worked on her USD. She credits this one strategy with launching her into an international business.

USD is different from branding. For a start, the cost of branding is prohibitively expensive for most small and medium businesses. Corporate giants such as Kellogg's, Gillette and perhaps the big daddy of them all, Coca Cola, spend billions of dollars maintaining their presence in the market. A lot of the advertising that you see for these companies is known as institutional advertising or image advertising – they are selling the company rather than a particular product. They don't really need to say what the product is anymore because that brand is so strong that it is synonymous with the product!

Let's say that we have a pen called the Corolla pen and you want your brand to be recognised as the best pen in the world. It's a new product so you dedicate five years to building the brand. The problem is unless you have a wealthy billionaire investor backing your new pen, you'll almost certainly go broke! If, on the other hand, you put an ad in the paper or put together a mailing campaign extolling the virtues of the Corolla pen, you will be able to sell the pen. Because you're selling a product, not a brand or concept, you can measure the success of the campaign and can fine tune your pitch to maximise your selling opportunities. This is direct response marketing and really is much more cash rewarding than institutional marketing.

Branding is way too broad to be of any real value to the small and medium business owner. So forget about it. Direct response on the other hand is a licence to print money and is much more important for a small or medium business owner. Direct response is anything that initiates a direct response. So an ad in the paper with a strong call to action would be direct response, as would a personalised letter to someone's door. Of course, you have to do it the right way. You have to know how to write really good copy that actually produces a result. You have to know the system and the good news is there is one – actual scientific principles that produce tangible results.

All you have to do is discover your Unique Selling Distinction and position your message in front of the right audience and wait for the money to flow in.

And the trick to all this is – be specific. Don't try to be all things to all people, especially in today's discerning market place. People want to know that you know who they are and that you appreciate their unique perspective. Whether that is genuinely a unique perspective or not is irrelevant – that's what makes them buy.

People want to feel understood and appreciated and they want to know that you understand their unique needs. You have to differentiate yourself in your market to meet the specific demands of niche audiences. That means you need to step into your customers' shoes and work out what they really want and position your business to meet that need.

Let me give you a classic example. I have a client who is an electrician and he was pretty sure that there wasn't a starving crowd for his services! Let's face it, not many people wake up in the morning desperate to meet an electrician. It's a service and not a particularly sexy one at that. It's a necessity more than a want, so how do you create a starving crowd for that business?

One of the ways to do this is to look at what your customers traditionally hate about your business – and solve it. So in the case of my electrician friend I asked him what most people hate about electricians. He sprang forth with a few suggestions including one about all tradesmen which was that they never arrived on time. How frustrating is that? They say they will arrive first thing and you're left wasting your entire day waiting for them and they never show up!

So we positioned him in the market accordingly. He promised that if he didn't arrive on time there was nothing to pay. It was on all his advertising and his business cards and it created a starving crowd because that was something that people got really upset about. Of course, he had to make sure he could manage his time and live up to that promise but he could and his business benefited. His business took off because of this one thing alone. Notice we didn't position him as 'the best electrician'. If we said that in the marketing no one would have believed it, and besides it is too broad. We positioned him in a very narrow way and it paid big results. We gave people what they wanted!

I also had client who is a plumber who was in a similar situation and wanted to increase his customers. We went through the same process and he identified that people were upset about the mess that plumbers sometimes left in the house. One of the things people hate about tradesmen is them tramping through their house in muddy boots. So he positioned himself as 'leaving your house cleaner than I found it – guaranteed'. Again this was a huge concern for people so when he visited someone's house he would remove his shoes at the door and put on a pair of plastic slippers. He had a mini vacuum cleaner and would vacuum his work area before he left to ensure that he left the house as clean or cleaner than when he found it.

Do you think that created a starving crowd? Do you think that set him apart and increased his client numbers? You better believe it did.

You can't be all things to all people so find your unique selling distinction and stand out on issues that are really important to your prospective client. In my case, I could be described as a business consultant but the market for that is, at best, mildly hungry. Doing this same process for myself I knew both from my own experience and other business owners that the biggest fear and biggest dream is money. So I position myself as 'the guy who puts more money in your pocket'. And that's exactly what I do!

To be really clear here, I'm not talking about 'spin' where you make something bad sound good and I'm not talking about lying to get customers. I'm talking about finding a way to speak to your customers in a way that connects to their deepest hopes and dreams. And deliver on that promise every time!

To help you think about your USD consider the following ideas …

Durability or quality

Remember the KingG slogan for working overalls, 'any tougher and they'd rust'. They were drawing the customer's attention to the product's durability. That was their USD. They didn't try and convince buyers they were sexy or stylish, they went for durability and that's what they are known for to this day. RM Williams uses a similar idea. RM Williams boots are known for their durability and they will easily last ten years. RM Williams also personifies the rugged masculine cowboy idea.

Price

This is a risky card to play in terms of your USD and I wouldn't recommend competing on price alone. Price is rarely what buying decisions come down to. The customer might say it's about the price but in my experience it's not always about the price. If you position yourself as the 'cheapest' you have to maintain that over time and that becomes your competitive strategy. There are many more lucrative ways to do business. Competing on price also tends to attract a certain type of customer – usually not the type you want!

Convenience

Another USD opportunity is around the idea of 'convenience'. You can buy it at our store or online and we will deliver it to your home. Or one of our sales representatives will come around and do a free quote.

The modern world is set up for speed and convenience. If there is a way that you can help people and make their life easier they will respond to that. People are pressed for time, this is a big headache for a lot of people. Remember, solving headaches is a great way to make money!

For example, one of the big irritations about getting your

car serviced is that you have to get your car to the garage and then you can't get to where you need to go next. So if a garage was to offer to take you to work, service your car while you were there and deliver it back to your work at the end of the day – how happy would you be? That would be a USD.

Delivery promise

Another USD is delivery time. Dominoes Pizza revolutionised the pizza delivery business because they found out what people hated most about ordering pizza – waiting forever for it to arrive – and solved it! They guaranteed that if your pizza didn't arrive within 30 minutes it would be free! That USD made them one of the most successful fast food companies in the world.

Service

Another option would be finding something unique about your service. Say, for example, you sold cars. The product and price may be much the same between you and your competitors but perhaps you were able to offer an after sales service that would set you apart. Making yourself just a little different and a little better can be all that's needed to clinch the deal.

Your USD should imply a specific benefit that the would-be customer is going to love. If possible it should be a one-line benefit statement. If you don't stand out then what you are is just one tree in a mighty forest. You've got to be the tree that's different. You've got to be the orange tree in a green forest. Now, not everybody likes orange trees, some people hate orange trees, but there is always going to be a market for people who just love orange trees. It's better to have a large slice of the orange tree loving market than battle for a miniscule slice of the green tree market! And you don't have to limit yourself to one niche market. You can position your offering to appeal to purple tree lovers or blue tree lovers too. You've just got to be different otherwise you're just another green tree in a continent of green trees. And that's hard work! You've got to differentiate yourself and stand out.

The mistake people make is they don't want to alienate anyone so they try to appeal to everyone. The other mistake they make is making their USD too generic like, 'we give the best service'. According to whom? This sort of statement doesn't work. I remember driving behind a removals van and their USD was, 'we give better service than anybody else'. It's meaningless. All you're left thinking is who else? Besides we don't believe that sort of statement because there is nothing specific and concrete about it. It's not a USD.

If I'm a plumber and I fix your toilets better than anybody in the area, who cares! I might care, on the other hand, if I said I was a plumber and you get a 60% discount on your first consultation – that's a USD. That's unique, I don't know any plumbers that are offering half price on a first consultation! Normally they charge you an arm and a leg before they've even looked at the problem! Most people wouldn't do it because they are thinking short term but if they thought about converting people into long-term customers it might work.

My USD for the courses I run is that I give business owners practical cash-generating strategies that work. I say that I will show you how to make a lot of cash out of a business and that's exactly what I do. You can check out the success stories on the website www.RichesFromBusiness.com. That's a USD because it's very clear and specific and it's what business owners want.

Write down ideas for your unique selling distinction
Think specifically about the things people hate about your profession. Think also about the problems your product or services solve. What's different about you and your business? And always think specifics, generalities have no power.

....

....

....

....

....

....

Big Results from a Small Advertising Budget

Now you have discovered your USD, understood the power of positioning your offering to multiple niche markets rather than the mass market, you are ready to cut your teeth on some advertising …

I do an exercise in one of my seminars that leaves people floored. It shows them how most advertising is a complete waste of money. We then show them how to create big results from a small advertising budget using a system that is easy and simple to implement.

When it comes to business success there are two different strategies that you can employ. First, you can wait for success to track you down and bang on your door. Or you can go out and find success and announce your arrival! One way is proactively getting involved in your success and driving your business to where you want it to be, and the other is reactive. Advertising, if done correctly, is very proactive. And the right way to advertise is the AIDA Formula.

The AIDA Formula

A stands for Attention

You've got to get your prospective customers' attention – or as I call it, 'creating a throat grabber headline'. You've got to create a headline that grabs them around the neck and stops them in their tracks so you can actually communicate with them.

I stands for Interest

Your ad has to create interest. There has to be a series of actual benefits for the prospective customer. The only way to create interest for someone is to relate it to WIIFM – 'what's in it for me'. There is a huge difference between a benefit and a feature. A feature is something that is good about a product; a benefit is what it actually does for them. Your advertising should focus on benefits (when I look at most advertising this doesn't occur).

D stands for Desire

Once you've grabbed their attention and captured their interest you have to create a desire for the product or service you are offering. You want to move the customer along from just noticing you to wanting what you have to offer. You need to engage them in what you will do for them and they have to start imagining themselves with your product or service.

A stands for Action

You've got to ask them to act – there has to be a call for action. I've seen some great written ads ruined by some tiny little phone number you can barely read. You've got to make it obvious, easy and urgent. Call immediately, call now. You have to have a specific call to action or a way that people can contact you. None of this is theoretical. There have been numerous tests where they put the phone number in and then later put the same ad with 'call now' before the phone number. The second one pulls more leads.

Immediately evaluate all your advertising pieces from the AIDA perspective.

A: Do you have an arresting, compelling headline? The headline should preferably work on calling attention to a problem or make a promise.

I: Straight after the headline you need to create an interest so that the reader will keep reading. The headline must grab their attention but the body copy must pull them in and keep them interested. Remember the #1 marketing sin is being boring.

D: Is you advertising creating a desire to buy? Once you've got their attention and kept them interested in what you are offering, is the advert creating a desire for your product or service? If not, people won't take action.

A: Do you have a strong call to action? Statistics show you have to create a specific direction to follow. 'Call today' or 'Pick up the phone right now'. Does your marketing tell your customer exactly what they need to do and give them a few options of contact? Not everyone likes making phone calls, so give people some options to order such as call a hotline, order online or a coupon to complete and post back.

You may not be the best person to decide if your marketing efforts hit the AIDA target – especially if you created them! It can be easy to fall in love with your own product, and certainly it's helpful if you are passionate about your business and what it sells, but most people are not as excited as you are. So constantly say to yourself 'so what!' to remind yourself to look for the hook. For example, I've seen so much advertising talking about how the business has been in operation for 25 years. So what! That doesn't necessarily mean anything until you convert it into language that the customer is going to be interested in. Putting the focus on the client, not the business, can make a boring statement much more powerful.

The Powerful Low Cost Technique to Dramatically Increase Sales

It is vital when you advertise to enter the conversation the buyer is already having in their mind. This is a really important part of marketing because if you don't address the sceptics straight up they won't get involved with you. One of the best ways to blast though all those concerns in one go is through risk reversal ...

Risk reversal is an extremely powerful concept, which ensures that any risk involved in choosing you over a rival business is removed. Say that you went to a restaurant and you had a really bad meal or the experience did not live up to the expectation or price tag. Most people would feel comfortable raising the issue with the restaurant and would expect a discounted or free meal.

And yet that same expectation doesn't translate into all businesses. In your business, if somebody complained, what would you do? The sensible thing would be to refund

the customer and bend over backwards to make amends –
especially if you were truly at fault.

That is the smart thing to do – simply because one angry
customer can make a lot of noise and it's never worth it. So if
you are happy to refund them if they are unhappy with your
product or service, why not tell them that up front!

Essentially that is all risk reversal is. It's assuring customers
and potential customers that should their experience of your
business fall short in any particular way that you will ensure
they are compensated. That way there is no risk involved for
the customer.

What I do and what I would advise you to think about
is to introduce a money-back guarantee on your product or
service. For example, on one of the courses I currently run I
offer a double-your-money-back guarantee! Yes, you read that
correctly. They get double the amount back that they paid!
As yet no one has asked for their money back because I
deliver. However, the offer is so compelling that a lot of
people buy because it immediately allays a lot of their fears.
Apart from allaying the inherent fears of your potential
new customer, it also ensures that you and your business
become dedicated to delivering the best possible service. If
you are confident that you are offering the best product
and service in your area then put your money where your
mouth is!

There is a real estate agency in the area where I live. It's the
number one agency in town. Why? Probably because there is
a sign in the window that states, 'If you are unhappy in any
way when we sell your house we will refund one hundred

percent of our commission'. Does that create more or less trust in the mind of the consumer?

And that's what risk reversal is all about – removing all the risk that your customers may experience when deciding whether or not to do business with you. This is especially important for attracting new customers as they have not experienced your business yet and don't know if it's a good choice or not. What you are trying to do is take the risk away from your client and put it on yourself. And let's face it, you will have to do that anyway because an unhappy client is far more destructive to your reputation than a happy one. It's just not good business sense NOT to fix an unhappy customer.

A great way of working out what your risk reversal should be is to find out what your customers are most scared of. Or find out what they hate about getting a business like yours involved in their life!

We talked about this earlier in terms of finding your Unique Selling Distinction (USD) but it's worth looking at it again from the perspective of honing your risk reversal proposition in order to attract new customers to your business.

You've got to be specific as to what you will do for them and how you do this. To do this you have to stand in your customer's shoes and ask yourself, 'If I were the client coming to my business what would my biggest fear be? If you find out what upsets people or what they like least about your business – and solve that problem – you immediately remove all the normal objections for getting involved.

For example, let's go back to tradesmen. One of the things people, especially women (and me for that matter), really hate is calling in a tradesman and having them mess up their home. They end up leaving more mess than there was when they started. They also hate not knowing what the cost will be until the workmen are in the house, by which time the customer has already incurred a cost! Imagine putting a risk reversal or a money-back guarantee that if we come in and do the plumbing, or we fix the electricity in your house and we leave the house dirtier than when we first came in, you get all your money back. That would be a specific risk reversal. Imagine if you add the fact that there will be no charge up front until you assess the cost and give them a quote and timeline. If they don't stick to that quote and timeline then the work is free!

The real power of the idea is that allays your customer's fears up front. If the tradesman does still leave a mess, although it's less likely if they are focused on being clean, you'd give a full refund straight away anyway because the alternative is just shortsighted. Even if the customer is 'wrong' – you'd still issue the refund and just make sure you never go back. It's not worth it any other way because we all know one angry customer can do more damage than 100 happy ones can repair.

By standing in the customer's shoes you can probably think of a number of aspects of your product or service that traditionally irritates customers and cater to them! Here are some suggestions to get you thinking about your business …

Find out what your customers dislike the most and remove the possibility of that experience. Risk reversal is a great way of getting potential customers over the line. After that you just have to make sure you deliver!

People always ask me, 'Is there a danger that there are people who simply take advantage of that?' Yes, of course there is. In fact there is absolutely no doubt that someone will take advantage of it. There are people that will abuse the system, but take the higher ground and make it easy for people to experience your product or service. You may get ripped off once or twice but the reality is that most people are honest. And for the occasional person that does abuse the system, fifty more may have bought from you that would never have bought unless there was a money back guarantee – it's a numbers game!

Risk reversal is a brilliant way to stand out. So few companies are really prepared to put their money where their mouth is and do this. Yet promoting your risk reversal as part of your marketing sends a very clear message to the customers that you stand by your product or service and that you are prepared to back that up with more than just words! People love that and if it's a choice between a company that offers a money-back risk reversal versus someone who doesn't – who do you think gets the new business?

Write down how you could create a specific money back guarantee relevant to your product or service.

Testimonial Marketing – A Rarely Understood Profit Generator

Testimonial marketing is very powerful because people are more likely to believe someone else's opinion about your business than your own.

If you are a plumber, for example, and you are deciding whether or not to buy a certain product or service you will be positively influenced if there is a recommendation or statement of support from another plumber.

Testimonial marketing can make a massive difference to your results and yet less than 2% of people use it. But just think about it for a second …

Who do you respect more – someone talking about how good they are or someone else talking about how good that person is? It's much more powerful when you hear a recommendation from someone else. Otherwise it just sounds like you're blowing your own trumpet! Plus, people don't necessarily believe you.

I have seen people use this one strategy and significantly increase their income in a matter of weeks.

The easiest way to show you how to do this is by giving you three of my recent testimonials and then show you the PRECISE formula you need to use.

'In just a few short months Brendan Nichols took us from a struggling business to an extraordinary success. His brilliant strategies produced sold out shows, time after time.

Our business has literally taken off and our profits have dramatically escalated. If you want someone who knows the fast track to success, he is the guy.'

Pia Almarker, Almarker Designs
VIC, Australia

'I used Brendan Nichols' Advanced Cash Generation System and created a mind blowing result. I wrote a single marketing piece that brought in 28 joint venture partners, each of whom are offering me between $30,000 to $100,000 to invest in my property ventures. I was amazed that I could generate such a huge amount of money in such a short time. After three days I had to withdraw the offer because the response was so great. I believe that it would be almost impossible for anyone in business to use these incredible techniques and not get amazing results that created more money and profits.

The system has so many other many tips and techniques; I just can't wait to try them all.'

Nora Surya, Property Investor, Melbourne

'Just one idea from Brendan Nichols led to an additional 1.1 million dollars profit within that calendar year.'
Tony McChesney, Director,
Compaction Australia

Okay, let me show you the formula you need to use.

First of all a testimonial has to be specific. It is no point having a testimonial that says, 'XYZ Company gave good service'. What does that mean? It's not specific enough so it sounds weak and wishy-washy. Because of the lack of specificity it's also unbelievable.

The examples above are specific. They have qualified or quantified the improvement they experienced in their respective businesses following my training. They also specify the time it took to achieve those results making it even more detailed – and as a consequence even more powerful.

The second element of a powerful testimonial is that it has to be measurable, notice how these testimonials fit this requirement. Avoid words like 'better' or 'great' unless they are accompanied by measurable evidence to prove that opinion and give the reader a benchmark for relevance.

Third – it has to include the full name, location, business and title of the person. Why? Because statistics show that most people do not believe a testimonial with initials. It looks made up. And just to clarify here I am not advocating that you make them up. Testimonials have to be from genuinely happy clients and if you don't have any of them then you have a whole world of problems that you need to tackle first!

Most businesses do have happy customers, they just never ask those happy customers for a testimonial. So my challenge to you is go out and get two testimonials. Ask the person involved if they could be as specific as possible and make sure you let them know how you intend to use what they write. Make it a habit to get customers to provide these so you can build up a portfolio of testimonials that you can use depending on your marketing and your target audience.

Let people know that you intend to use them on your website or marketing and make sure they are happy with that. Then once you have them use them ... don't sit them in a drawer to have a look at when you're feeling a little blue. Tell the world about how happy your customers are; rotate them on your website so a new one pops up every time someone visits the site.

If you tell the world how great you are they may not listen, but if you have an army of happy customers doing that for you, you will be amazed at what that does for business.

The Power of Bonus Selling

The power of bonus selling is a great technique for harnessing extra cash.

As human beings we hate to miss out on stuff. So when someone says to us we have to act before a certain time frame, or that there is only 14 left, this knowledge activates the psychological driver of scarcity. And marketers have used this to great effect. This is what they are doing when they offer products and services which are available for a limited time only or perhaps they include a date after which you won't be eligible for the extra discount.

The principle works like this. First you offer something using the scarcity principle. Then you offer an additional bonus for them to act immediately. Why? Because you have to get that person to take action immediately otherwise they will put it aside to think about it. The reality, of course, is if they put it aside, they never go back to the offer and instead find it in the newspaper pile three months after the offer expired! People like to put things off – especially decisions that they are sitting on the fence about. So you need to make it as easy as possible for them to get off the fence and make a positive decision.

When we create scarcity AND add an additional bonus then we increase the chances of overcoming that resistance. That extra free gift is enough to activate the power of reciprocity and the limited availability of that extra value item is enough to move them into immediate action.

Here is how it works
1. Scarcity
2. Bonus
3. Scarcity

We make the offer, and then add a bonus that is only available if they take action within a certain time period.

It's likely that you will recognise this mix although you may not have necessarily known what it was. If you've ever seen those infomercials or those ads for 'steak knives' you would have seen this principle in action. The last part of the offer is 'ring in the next three minutes and get an additional bread knife or serrated vegetable slicer'. Or the first 25 callers get an additional gizmo. Whatever the offer is, the bonus is relevant to that offer and usually has a high-perceived value.

Many marketers have found that it is more effective to take something out of the offer and then offer the same product as an additional bonus. For example, let's say you were selling ten items in your offer. Try taking four items out of the offer and only selling six then offer those four additional items as bonuses. It is an extremely effective technique. The customer ends up with the same package but more often than not will feel better about their purchase and are less likely to suffer from buyer's remorse.

You need to look at your product portfolio and start getting creative about how you can bundle things together to attract new or more customers. How can you create or acquire additional bonuses to increase your selling success?

Think especially about information products ... these are simple to create and have a high-perceived value. For example, say you were a wedding cake decorator you could create an e-book called the 'Insiders Secrets of Inspired Cake Decorating' – simply by using some of the knowledge and experience you've acquired over your years in the profession, and you could offer your customers a great bonus. You get to promote your business by including pictures of your greatest creations, and your customers get something really helpful that could improve their own cake decorating. You can create an entirely new profit centre and for some business people it can be more lucrative than their current business.

Oh, and don't worry, you won't be doing yourself out a job. I often hear people ask, 'Why do you give so much information away? Shouldn't you hold some back so you stay the expert?' Or 'Surely if you give it all away they will be able to do what you do and won't need you anymore.' The reality is actually very different. For a start, unfortunately, statistics prove that most people will not do anything with the information anyway. But more importantly, one of the strangest things about giving people valuable information is that they become even more likely to seek your future assistance, not less. If you share your knowledge freely and genuinely try to help others instead of hoarding it and keeping your cards to your chest, you foster trust. And whether you're in a loving relationship or a buying relationship, trust is essential for longevity. So share your knowledge and try to help your customers save money or have a better life. You might be very pleasantly surprised.

A word of warning …

Some of these techniques can sound manipulative and they certainly can be if abused. I'm sharing them with you for two reasons. The first is so that you can see what others are doing to you and be a little more discerning about who you give your cash to and for what purpose. And the second is so that you can use them with integrity. If you don't have testimonials, don't make them up – improve your performance so you get them. These tools are powerful and will work again and again if you are delivering a quality product or service. If you're conning people you will only ever do it once and that's not the basis for long-term business success. Besides you still have to sleep at night, so treat people in the way you would wish to be treated. Make your offering the best it can be and find people that would genuinely benefit from it.

How a Tasmanian Tiger can put Cash in Your Pocket!

Local residents of Byron Bay were agog when the local rag ran a front-page story on how residents had spotted the extinct Tasmanian tiger! No one knows for sure whether it was a joke, but one smart entrepreneur cashed in! Before I tell you how he did it, and how you can replicate the idea for yourself and get loads of free publicity, let me tell you one of my pet peeves.

Considering our convict history I think it's fairly safe to say we live in a land that was built with a healthy disregard for authority. This is Australia, the lucky country and the land of Ned Kelly. But it seems to me that we are losing that maverick spirit and adopting a more 'play by the rules, look good and do as you're told' approach. Now don't get me wrong. I am not talking about robbing banks or breaking the law. I'm talking about lateral thinking and having some fun! You can be legal, moral and still operate with a maverick or renegade spirit.

If you want to be successful, without working yourself to the bone then you need to think outside the square. Do something different, be daring, boring doesn't sell.

So what did our intrepid entrepreneur do? His store is called Uncle Tom's Pies and not far from the alleged sightings of the 'tigers'. The very day the story broke in the papers he had a big sign made up and put it near his store. It read:

NEWSFLASH:
Tasmanian Tigers saved from extinction by eating Uncle Tom's pies.

His claim was that the tigers must have been eating all the leftovers out the back. However, it gets even better! He went and hired three young women, and had them pose in front of the sign with feigned looks of terror on their faces (think of those tacky 1950s horror movies). He then called the paper and guess which photo is running on the front page? The publicity he got was enormous, not to mention every resident talking and laughing about the whole thing. And what did it cost him? A couple of hundred bucks!

His strategy is a classic 'Publicity Strategy'. You take a hot media story and run a publicity campaign off it. I used a variation of this when I turned my first book into a bestseller. At the time when journalists were very sceptical of self-development books, I wrote a press release with the headline, 'Why Self Improvement Books Don't Work'. It immediately grabbed attention. I went on to explain where they didn't work and where they did (and why mine did). In other words – while most authors were fighting against the flow, I went with it. Success comes more easily when you swim downstream!

Another great example comes from the late John Ilhan of Crazy John's. Remember the TV show The Block, where four couples renovated a house and whoever made the most profit kept it? When the Bondi apartments in Sydney were complete and the auction was to be broadcast live on TV, John Ilhan had the idea to get someone to go to the auction and bid dressed as his mascot Crazy John … Crazy John's bought the best apartment and his business got millions in free publicity from the stunt.

How can you duplicate this? Start asking, 'What could I do differently'? How could I be more daring? How could I make money without having to spend a lot? What news story could I ride on the back of?'

The Power of 'Maximisation' – a Little Known Formula to Increase Your Success

Maximisation is all about increasing the amount of purchases from the customers or clients that you already have. This principle of maximisation can be a profit revolution for many businesses. It can also be somewhat of a revelation!

Say you had a hundred loyal clients who purchase from you twice a year. What would happen to your business if you could sell them something three times a year? That would be like finding an extra 33 new clients! Except new clients have a client procurement cost involved which will impact net profit. Selling more often to the clients you already have does not incur those associated costs. If you focused your attention on lifting sales regularity, even slightly, your business would go through the roof.

Don't be fooled by turnover. I hear this all the time, 'Yeah but I have a turnover of X'. Who cares what your turnover is – it's a meaningless number. All you're interested in is net profit. And that means making sales that don't cost money to make – and that means increasing the frequency that your existing customers buy from you. Think of the amount of extra profit you could generate by providing a way where your clients could purchase from you more often. And it doesn't have to be complicated …

Take my electrician friend. He could create a 'comfort check-up', an annual assessment of the home to ensure that all things electrical are safe for the family. This could include a smoke alarm test and an energy-saving tips booklet. He could source innovative energy-saving products or services and let his customers know of the next big thing through a regular email newsletter. He may even be able to negotiate a strategic alliance with these product manufacturers so he can supply them and create another stream of income. And if he really establishes trust, he can sell them products that are totally unrelated to his field. You need to start thinking creatively about what the market wants or could be convinced they want, and how you can meet that need.

Where are you making your money?

Few businesses really analyse where they make the bulk of their money. If it comes in that's good enough for them and any analysis is seen as time-consuming and futile. But it's just another version of the Pareto principle – if you were to look you'd probably find that 20% of your clients make 80%

of your revenue. If you looked you'd probably find that 20% of your products or services were accounting for 80% of your revenue.

Knowing where the bulk of the money comes from and when it arrives is crucial if you are to maximise your potential. When people refer to the 'front end' of a business, they are referring to the fact that most of their revenue is made at the beginning of the buying relationship. The front end of the business therefore refers to the initial products and services that are sold. They are often the ones that attract the customer in the first place.

For example, a jeweller may run television advertising focusing his offer on discount necklaces and rings. These would be regarded as a 'loss leader' because he knows that although he may lose on those purchases, he will attract more customers to his store so he can not only sell more products but also direct the customer to more or alternative purchases and higher-cost items.

How profitable is your front end and do you have a strategy?

Keeping the entry point low may mean a low profit margin or breakeven, but could result in a longer relationship and the on-going opportunity for repeat sales. Alternatively, if there is minimal opportunity for repeat sales then a different strategy may need to be adopted. Many businesses, if truth be told, don't have a strategy and are selling products willy nilly with no thought of how best to foster the buying relationships and engage the customer in a long-term relationship.

Write down your strategy. What are you trying to achieve? Do you want volume or are you interested in lower-volume high-margin?

The Powerful 'Selling After You've Sold' Technique

If the front end is all about what you sell at the start, the back end is all about selling once you've already sold. A back end is an additional product or service that is sold to a client after you have attracted them with your front end proposition.

One example of a back end is life insurance. The initial purchase may be at a low profit to the agent, however, once the agent has a client they are able to develop the relationship and build trust so that they can then offer other types of insurance, which the customer may need and which may be more profitable. I have seen businesses massively increase their profitability by adding just one back end product or service.

Remember, it is very expensive to get a customer however if you have a loyal customer or client then it is much easier and less expensive to get them involved with additional products or services. This makes your life and theirs a lot easier.

Do you have an existing back end strategy? Write it down.

Can additional back end products be created?

The answer is almost always yes, and this one area alone can transform your business into a money-making machine. Let's say you owned a mail-order business that sold a particular face cream. That product attracted a high re-order and consequently you had a loyal customer base for that product. All you need to do is enclose a flyer with other related beauty products. Include a 'specially selected discount coupon' with the flyer for all orders before a certain date and your sales will increase. This is also known as an up-sell or cross-sell and it's a really powerful way to make more money with very little effort.

A friend of mine, Paul, owned a video shop and he's a really smart guy. He had weekly videos that rent for $3 or you could rent five for $8. In the course of the day his customers would come in and grab a weekly DVD for $3 and walk up to the counter. All Paul said was, 'Have you heard about our special?' That's a great line – very non-confrontational. If the customer said no, which they nearly always did, then he said, 'You can get this for $3 but you can get five for $8.' More often than not the person would think that was a good deal because they are weeklies and so they thought they would have time to watch them. They went and chose four other movies.

Most people would never get around to watching all five, but Paul knew they were better sitting on his customers' shelves than his! The customer felt like they were getting a good deal and a big discount on what it would have cost to rent five videos and the Paul was making an extra $5 because he knew without the deal not many would rent five movies. Everyone was happy. And from saying one little sentence at the checkout, Paul added an extra six figures a year to his business!

The really interesting part to this story is that Paul decided to sell his business. The new owner didn't feel comfortable reminding the customer of the five film offer, so he never asked. He lost thousands of dollars in that business as a result. Remember, it's much easier and cheaper to sell to an existing client than it is to get a new client.

When you are thinking about creating new back end opportunities or up-sells, you need to think about it from a few perspectives. Currently you are providing your existing products to your existing markets. That may be working fairly well but you need to think bigger.

The first way to view this idea is to look at existing products/new market. What do you have already have that could be re-packaged or re-positioned to meet the demands of a new or niche audience? A classic example of this is the Sony Walkman. Originally, a very similar product was sold to journalists as a recording device. All Sony did was remove the recording device and add some speakers and re-position it as music-on-the-move and a phenomena was created. Sony created a market that wasn't even there by honing in on a desire that most people didn't even know they had!

The second perspective to explore is new product/existing

market. Is there scope in your capabilities to increase your product offerings so that your current clients have more options to buy from you? Books by famous authors are a good example of this. For some people it doesn't matter what he writes, they will always buy a Stephen King book. He is constantly creating new products to keep his existing market happy. The same can be said for many successful authors.

The third perspective is new products/new markets. Say, for example, you are a florist and competing with every other florist in the area. You need to stand out, so you could re-package what you already do to meet the needs of a niche group. Think outside the square ... what about offering to deliver dead flowers as a break-up gift! Believe it or not there is now a website and booming business in the US that does just that! How good is that, the florist sells what is unsellable and makes money from a liability! Personally I think it's a weird thing to do, but it's a brilliant idea. The florist could also look at his or her location and cash in on a particular demographic. For example, if you owned a florist on Oxford Street you could position yourself as the gay wedding flower specialist. If you wanted new products you could source really exotic and unusual flowers and position yourself as the florist that sells flowers that do actually say something! You could even take it a step further and create poems or verses that go with each rare flower to say a special something.

That's all Hallmark cards have done – you can get a card now that says just about everything. Every conceivable relationship or connection is now captured in Hallmark cards!

Write down how you could maximise your clients. Remember it is easier to work with your current clients than to get new clients. You need to be constantly focused on up-selling, cross-selling and repeat purchases. Up-selling is when your existing clients are offered more expensive products or services. Cross-selling is getting them to buy other products or services in your range. And repeat purchases are about increasing the amount of times your customers buy your staple products or service. So think about what you have already and what you could easily create without a huge investment. Brainstorm with your team and really pay attention to your customers. Ask the team to be on the lookout for new ideas and to take note of any customer suggestions. Often it is those people habitually using your product or service who could provide you with some great suggestions – if you just asked or listened.

What other existing products do you have that you could sell to your existing customers?

....

....

....

....

....

....

....

What new products/services could you create to appeal to your existing customers?

....

....

....

....

....

....

....

....

....

....

What existing products/services could you repackage or re-position to appeal to a new market?

....

....

....

....

....

....

What new products/services could you repackage or reposition to a new customer?

FA$T 15

Beware the Gold Watch Salesman

It's important to maximise your sales skills and sales force, however, before you go trying to turn everyone in your business into a cross between a rabid Doberman and an Amway rep on espresso, beware the gold watch salesman …

Being good in sales is not about high-pressure cold calls or anything else that makes your blood run cold. It's about people and relationships. I don't think there is a person alive that enjoys being sold to. I remember one experience that really brought home to me just how wrong people can get it when it comes to the all-important areas of sales.

I had spent all afternoon shopping for an expensive watch and I was getting really frustrated. My frustration wasn't with the watches but the people selling them.

Let me introduce you to some of the characters in my bizarre shopping adventure. This is a kind of 'Fawlty Towers' version – do the opposite of this and you will make more money. The fact is, everyone I know who is rich and successful is good at sales. It's very important so spend some time getting it right and understand how it goes wrong …

Character 1: The Shark

The first salesperson was bored. He remained bored until I mentioned the words, 'solid gold'. It was like I had simultaneously pumped him with adrenaline and given him electric shock treatment. Immediately I had a new best friend. I felt like I was in a cartoon where Daffy Duck just showed up and has dollar signs rolling in his eyes like the barrel of a slot machine. Lesson 1 – Never look at someone with dollar signs in your eyes. No one likes to be treated like a commodity.

Character 2: The Hearing-Impaired Salesperson

The next tragic sales effort was from an eager young man who was convinced that I needed the latest piece of fashion. I wanted a watch but he strapped something to my wrist that looked like you could land aircraft on it. It was huge and I was reminded of Oscar Wilde who said, 'Fashion is something so ugly it needs to be changed every three weeks.'

My cries for 'sleek, elegant and stylish' were drowned out in his quest to turn me into a rapper with a giant piece of bling. Find out what your customer wants and give them that, as opposed to finding out what you want to sell and forcing it on them! It sounds simple and yet it's staggering how few businesses get this right.

Character 3: The Wimp

Next up was a well-meaning young woman whose response to all my comments was, 'well if you don't like it, I am sure we could lower the price!' Who wants to buy something that they don't want, at any price? It's wimpy to always use price as a bargaining chip. It's also stupid. I was buying an expensive watch – if price was an issue I wouldn't be buying an expensive watch. Do you think Ferrari negotiate on price?

Lesson 3 – Take the time to find out what your customer really wants and more importantly why they want it. The only way to help anyone is to find out what they want not what you think they want. This applies not only to sales but all your marketing.

If you were to announce that you were changing your business and you wanted to instil a selling culture you'd have a mutiny on your hands. Most people are terrified of sales so don't alarm them unduly. Just start changing the systems to ensure that people receive a consistently good service. If you think back to my friend Paul in the video store, he wasn't hard selling, he was just consistently asking one simple question. That's all it takes to instil a selling culture into your team.

Make it easy for your team and make it easy for your

customers to buy even a little bit more from you a little more often.

The four vital steps to keeping customers

So once you've worked your socks off to get your marketing right, get the right systems and make sure you are consistently delivering something the market wants, you need to KEEP those customers.

These are the four vital steps to ensure you do...

STEP 1

Under-promise and over-deliver. Most people get this mixed up and they end up over-promising and under-delivering. Tell them what you are going to do and do it! But do it better, faster or to a higher quality than they could ever have hoped for. Surprise and delight your customers. It is so easy to stand out from the pack just doing this alone. So few businesses

256

actually deliver what they promise – make sure yours is one of them!

STEP 2

Tell them. There is no point delivering above and beyond the call of duty if the customer is completely oblivious to it!

I have a friend whom I consider to be one of the best masseurs and bodyworkers in the world – and he has over 60 different healing and bodywork techniques. Unless he told people that, no one would know. I remember first meeting him and being so impressed by that. I know a lot of bodyworkers and perhaps they have studied half a dozen, or ten techniques, but I've never met anybody that has studied 60. Unsurprisingly enough, this guy is an absolute master. He's phenomenal and because he tells people about all his training, people are more than happy to pay $300 an hour, which is considerably more than your masseurs who may be charging about $60 or $80. You have got to tell people what you've done, not only in terms of your experience and what you bring to the table, but you have to tell them when you deliver a great service. If your guys have worked through the night to make this happen – tell your customer. You don't have to make a song and dance about it, but just let your clients know when you went the extra mile for them.

STEP 3

Be part of your community. I remember meeting a girl called

Candy and she had a little coffee shop in Manly. The food was just above average but her unique selling distinction was solely around creating community and family, a place where people belonged. She knew everyone's name and was like everyone's Mum. Create a feeling of community and people will turn up, people will want to be part of your community. Everybody wants to belong to something.

STEP 4

Fall in love with your customer or client, not your product or service. Most people are so enamoured with their product they actually forget who's buying it. For example, I consulted a real estate company one time and I asked them how sales were. They said that they were not really selling anything except a particular block of units. I asked them more about these units and it turned out that everyone in the real estate office loved this development. It was right on the river and really represented where these guys really wanted to be. My response to them was, 'Who cares what you like?' Their subconscious predisposition toward that particular development was translating into great sales but why couldn't they get that excited about their other properties?

Their sheer passion for the apartment block was pulling in a few customers but when they would show potential buyers a house in the 'burbs' they had no passion because it wasn't the kind of place where they wanted to live themselves. And so, people just weren't buying. I said to them, what you have to do is establish your customer's need. It's not about what you love, it's about what your customer loves!

It's like the guy in the watch shop trying to sell me a landing strip for my arm. He didn't hear what I said; he didn't respect my choice enough to show me things that I wanted. Instead he showed me watches that he thought were nice.

Your job isn't to force your product or service onto people. Your job is to find out what people want and need and see who of those people could be helped by your product or service! It's not about you – it's about them!

So, it's about falling in love with your customers or clients. You have got to find out what your clients want. If you still don't know what they want, ask them.

Write down specifically your action plan for what you are going to promise to your customers.

....

....

....

....

....

Foster a Culture of Customer Care

One of the best ways to ensure on-going happy customers is to foster a culture of customer care. You need to have people in your business that are prepared to do whatever it takes to meet the demands and needs of your valued customers.

And note I said valued customers. Bending over backwards for tyre-kickers isn't beneficial so I'm not talking about those customers that consume huge amounts of time and spend tiny amounts of money. Find the real customers, the ones that are genuinely interested in your product or service and are happy to pay for it – you need to look after them. They are the diamonds in your business.

Commit to a level of service that you can handle and make it happen. Do what you say you will do and keep your promises. When there are delays or mistakes, be honest. Get on the phone and fix it. And that means having everyone in the business on board. Empower people to fix your customer challenges quickly. You can still surprise and delight an unhappy customer and if you do, you might be surprised to know they become even more loyal. People don't expect perfection all the time but they want to be kept informed and told the truth. 'I'm sorry' really does go a long way!

It's easy to think that business is a faceless entity, but it's not. People do business with people they like. Businesses are a collection of human beings and as such they are governed by human characteristics. Those characteristics dictate that those looking for a product or service would rather sacrifice a little on cost or quality to do business with someone they can trust and they like.

How can you improve customer goodwill (a vital asset)?

The Secret of Cutting Expenses or Overheads

This is self-explanatory and is an important part of putting more cash in your pocket.

Keeping control of your expenses is an important aspect of business success and is perhaps the only thing that doesn't fall within the income time or busy time bracket.

I will make this really simple. Look at everything you spend and ask the question, 'Do we really need to do this and does it increase our profitability?'

Don't confuse this for becoming tight with your money. This is not about laying-off staff and getting those left to pick up the slack, this is about paying your people well and finding ways to make the business process more efficient and cost-effective.

A great way to find these efficiencies is to empower your team to find them. When International Harvester was in trouble, they offered some of their subsidiaries the opportunity for a leveraged buy-out. Jack Stack and 12 senior managers took up the offer and bought the bankrupt-bound Springfield Remanufacturing Corporation (SRC). That was in 1983 and since then SRC has grown into 22 separate companies with a combined revenue of over 120 million dollars. Many of those new businesses are the direct result of employees identifying company weaknesses and finding solutions to them. The business was re-created under the leadership of Stack and his team and they created what is now known as The Great Game of Business – an open book management philosophy that truly empowers employees and gives them a say and a slice of profitability.

So ask your people what they would do to improve the efficiency of their particular job, look at how viable the suggestions are, and then implement the best ones.

How can I cut down on expenses?
Make a list of all the unnecessary overheads and expenses. Most business owners only do this when things get tight. The best time to do it is before things get tight. Trim the fat!

Develop a Business That is a Saleable Asset to Create a Big Windfall

You need to know first if you have a business that can be sold.

Looking at this, it is clear that not all businesses have the potential to be a saleable businesses. Say you are a specialised computer technician. You may be the most advanced computer technician of that type on the planet. But it wouldn't translate into a saleable business. I sometimes call it the Picasso effect. Picasso was very successful at selling his paintings but he didn't have a saleable business because he was the business. As soon as Picasso left the business, there was no business.

If, on the other hand, you do have a business that is not dependent on your expertise or particular skill set, then you may have a saleable asset. But this is something that is best considered early on. If you have already established your business then you need to turn your focus to creating a saleable entity.

It also means that you will need to focus on systemising your business and being able to prove that there is a proper business structure in place. And would-be buyer wants assurances that your results are duplicable, otherwise the investment is far too risky. The would-be buyer also wants to know that he or she can bring in their team and get them up to speed ASAP so that the momentum is not lost in the transition period. Systemised policies and procedures ensure that's possible.

Is it possible to set up your business to sell it in the future? If so, write down what you need to do to accomplish this.

Make it Happen ... The Easy 3-Step Strategic Plan

To be successful you need to have a plan or strategy. It doesn't always mean you will rigidly adhere to your strategy (sometimes you need a little flexibility) but to climb the pinnacle of success, you do need to map out a plan.

What I am going to give you is a very powerful but simple formula that will help you master the law of strategy. This formula is called 3-step strategic thinking. Before I give you the formula, let me tell you why it is so important and why unsuccessful people don't use it.

The problem with most business owners, employees and people in general is they get stuck in the day-to-day grind. They have a 'to do list' and just keeping up with this occupies their entire time. Having a 'to do' list is extremely important. You need to keep appointments, return phone calls and answer emails but that is just part of the picture. But if all you ever do is just work on your list, then there is no time to plan your future. If you have ever played chess you will know that a poor chess player thinks of their next move. An average chess player thinks one or two moves into the future. An extraordinary chess player thinks of their third or fourth move. They extend themselves even further to think of the possible moves they could take and have back-up plans and alternatives already mapped out.

It is exactly the same with people who attain an extraordinary level of success in the world. Successful people think and plan into the future. The easiest way to do that is to use the 3-step strategic thinking formula, where you think and act on three different levels.

Step 1. Immediate

Step 1 is to plan your immediate future. Let's use a very easy example. Imagine you owned a pastry shop. To plan the immediate future you would write a list or create a system where you ordered the flour and the other ingredients to make the pastries. You would organise all the day-to-day details that involved running that business.

Step 2. Intermediate

Step 2 is where you plan your intermediate future. These are projects that you want to get online in the next six to

12 months. Going back to our pastry shop – in six months time you might plan to add a catering service to the business or expand the size of the shop. It could also be things like looking at streamlining your systems, getting new leads or contracts.

Step 3. Future

Step 3 is where you plan your future. This is where you see the eventual outcome of what you started. It is the finished product. For example, you may have started that pastry shop with the sole idea that you wanted to build it up from nothing and then sell it in five years.

If you look at the 3-step process it is very similar to our extraordinary chess player, who thinks of their next move, then the next few moves and then right out into the future.

So where do you start? You begin with the final outcome. To use this formula effectively you work backwards from the future. The first fundamental question you ask yourself is, 'What is it that I ultimately want to create? What would my final outcome look like?'

If you want to really discover how important 3-step strategic thinking is, all you have to do is look at couples or relationships that are operating at Step 1, the immediate future. They are busy picking up the kids, rushing off to work and doing all the necessary day-to-day things. Ask them how the romance and passion is in their relationship and you will probably get a blank look. If they want to create an extraordinary relationship again and rekindle that passion and intimacy where they are each other's best friend, they need to plan for that and make it a priority. If that's their shared goal then how that comes about suddenly gets easier. The things they need to do to achieve that become almost obvious.

All three levels operate simultaneously. Imagine you are a world-class runner. Level 1 of strategic thinking would be your immediate training regime. How many kilometres will you clock up today? Level 2 would be focusing on that big track and field event that's coming up in three months time. Level 3 would be a clear picture of you, one day standing on the dais, holding the Olympic gold medal.

If you get stuck on level 1, you are on the treadmill of life. If you get to level 2, you might be placed in the track and field event but unless you start all your planning from the level 3 perspective, it's unlikely you'll make it. After all, would an athlete's training regime be different for a track and field event than it would be for the Olympics? You better believe it would be. Nothing is left to chance for an Olympic athlete, everything they eat, everything they do, is converging on that point.

The most successful people in the world think this way. Never let a day go by without using this powerful technique. Strategic thinking can lift you to your own gold medal so you can win your personal 'Olympics'. Whatever that may be.

Finding a Mentor Who Can Fast Track You

Back in the days when I owned my real estate company, I wanted to learn more about the financial and investment markets.

At the time, a major investment firm from Chicago had transferred a young, hotshot genius to the Sydney office. Tom became their chief analyst and had an extraordinary ability to forecast market trends. I contacted him, explained who I was and then offered him a deal that at first startled him before he finally accepted.

Here is what I did. For three weeks I became his personal assistant. I made his coffee, ran errands – you name it, I did it, AND I did it for no money! In return he began explaining everything he knew about the markets. The experience was priceless. I learned more in those three weeks about what REALLY worked than I could have in a year of university.

Not only that, but I was trading my account in direct

conjunction with all of Tom's trades and at the same time learning why he was doing what he was doing. One particular trade made me a 200% return on investment in 48 hours. And I had a lot of fun and accessed a world that is normally closed to outsiders.

It was a phenomenal experience and I've recommended it many times. I know at the time many people were extremely surprised at what I was doing. To them it was a step backwards from where I was and their reasoning was something like this: 'You are a highly successful businessman. How can you lower yourself to become someone's PA?'

This mentality stops a lot of people from exploring the idea of having a mentor. The ego rears its ugly head and people feel that they won't 'lower' themselves to learn from someone who has a greater skill base than them. This becomes even more pronounced as we get older. As an adult it's assumed or implied that we should know everything and the idea of learning from others seems unappealing.

And yet finding a mentor is one of the fastest ways to turbo-charge your success – in any area of your life. If you want to be financially successful, find someone who has become financially successful in the area you're in and learn from them. If you want to know how to have a long and happy marriage, find a couple who have had a long and happy marriage and ask them how they did it.

Here are some suggestions for finding a great mentor:

1.

Only choose someone who has been successful in the REAL world. There is an invisible energy that radiates from successful people. Just being around them creates a kinesthetic (feeling) learning that you can embrace. Be very careful about learning from anyone who hasn't 'got' that. In the end no intellectual qualification is a substitute for experience. Ideally a mentor would have both, but real world results are by far the most important measure when looking for someone suitable.

For example – if you want to be a really lousy golfer, come and learn from me. When it comes to golf, I definitely haven't got it.

2.

Find someone who loves to teach and can break it down for you. Kinesthetic learning is one part of the picture. You also need to learn the steps. If you have a mentor that loves the teaching process and loves to tell you how things work then you will learn so much more than someone you have to drag everything out of. It should be an enjoyable experience for everyone involved so find someone that really wants to teach.

3.

Ask. You would be surprised just how many people would love to help you – if you are willing to ask. These days, my schedule is so full that I rarely get the time to mentor one-on-one any more. However, I used to be amazed at how many people would approach me in a seminar and say something like, 'Wow, I'd love to know how you do that – is there anywhere I could study that?' I've had less than six people ask me to directly mentor them and guess what? I did. When I was first starting out, I never charged them a cent. Have the courage to ask – all they can say is no. If they do say no – keep looking and keep asking until someone says yes.

4.

Find a way to contribute to them. You need to exchange their mentorship and the value it offers you for something that could be of value to them. Offer some kind of service for their information. When I worked as a PA it was perfect for Tom because he was new to the city. I did all his running around and also was able to give him a real taste of the place and help him get settled in faster. The best way to find something of value is, again, to ask. Find out what they need and want. Maybe you could mow their lawn every weekend because they hate gardening. Maybe you could become their personal chauffeur and they could teach you as you drive. Come up with some other innovative way to show your appreciation and reciprocate the value they are showing you.

5.

Develop a deep gratitude for those who help you. There are several people who have helped me in my journey who hold a special place in my heart. There is a very interesting thing that happens to grateful people. They tend to attract people who want to help them. Two of the most important words in the English language are Thank You.

Business coaching has become increasingly popular in today's competitive world and part of the reason is because it's one thing to get on track but it's quite another to stay there. Life happens whether we like it or not, your plans can so easily be put on the backburner. Having a coach or mentor is a great way for you to stay accountable to your dreams and make sure that what you say is important, stays important.

Above all keep learning. Someone once said, 'If you think education is expensive, try ignorance!'

Conclusion

I can confidently assume that you bought this book because you were either sick of the rat race and want a way to get out, or you've got a business but the only person getting any benefit are your employees. I can also safely assume that, whatever your situation, you are at, or close to, your snap point and just want a way to 'get a life' and enjoy some financial prosperity at the same time. Or you're already successful and like all successful people you're constantly on the lookout for ways to keep you that way.

But it doesn't matter if you have a fleet of Ferraris and a Lear jet (or whether you want one) or whether you just want to be able to play golf a little more and hang out with your kids. Whatever your dreams are, your business can support them. It's all possible.

We've covered a lot in this book. First we looked at who you are and what it is you really want. We exposed some myths about money so you could feel a little more unencumbered about attaining and keeping lots of it! We looked at the options you have for its accumulation and introduced you to the idea that you are already a living expression of your success drivers although you may not have been aware of it. We also explored the concept of an income ceiling and that perhaps this invisible block is stopping you from achieving the level of success you crave. And just getting some awareness about how potent your psychology is in attaining your dreams is an enormously important lesson.

We looked at the difference between strategies and structure and took a closer look at the levels of wealth and the foundations of wealth. And we looked at the attributes necessary for wealth and the factors that can hold us back, such as the seven deadly sins of time. And finally, I explained 21 powerful Financial Acceleration $uccess Techniques for you to systematically incorporate into your business so you can truly enjoy the lifestyle you desire.

And you know what? I'm genuinely excited for you right now. Because I reluctantly accept that of the thousands of people that bought this book, about 5% will make it here. So if you're reading these words – congratulations. Your persistence is unusual and already sets you apart. And that's why I'm excited for you. Because you do have the tenacity to see things through to the end and that's all you really need in business. You need to stick with things and take action and adapt.

Everything you need to massively improve your business is written in these pages and you've already separated yourself from 95% of the population by reading to this point. Why not separate yourself still further and action what's in it!

Helen Keller once said, 'Life is either a daring adventure or nothing at all.' I love this quote not just because I absolutely agree with the sentiment but because of who said it. Helen Keller was an American author, activist and lecturer. She was the first deaf-blind person to graduate from college and in so doing changed the landscape of possibility for everyone in her situation who followed. Helen Keller's contribution to the world is enormous despite her 'handicap'.

Now I don't know your experiences and I don't know your challenges but I'm pretty sure that they are nothing like the challenges that Helen Keller faced. And yet she lived a daring adventure so if you don't, what's your excuse going to be?

What are you going to tell your grandkids when you are sitting on your rocking chair looking back over your life? Are you going to tell them it was a daring adventure or are you going to fill them with stories about how you could have been rich if it wasn't for blah blah blah?

You deserve to live the life that you dream about – whatever that is. Life is so short – we have about 4000 weeks. And said like that, it doesn't seem very many. So what are you going to do with them?

Are you going to stay in a job you hate because you think that it's your lot in life or are you going to open your eyes to the opportunities around you? Are you going to struggle on in your business doing the same things over and over again and wondering why nothing ever changes or are you going to take the strategies in this book and make some real money?

Are you going to wonder what it's like NOT to have money worries and what it must be like to be able to take several months off a year and enjoy some down time? Are you going to imagine what it would be like to drive a gorgeous car or learn how to ski or live in a fabulous house or are you going to use of few of those 4000 weeks and find out?

The life you live is your choice. Most people really don't want to face this fact. It's uncomfortable because it puts us squarely in charge of our results and our future. Certainly it's easier to be able to sit back and blame everything from the economy to politics to global warming for the fact that you're not reaching your potential but you and I both know the truth. If you're not living the life you desperately want, it's your choice. You may not have been aware of having made the decisions that resulted in your current situation, but you are now. How you live from this point forward is a choice.

So what's it to be? Are you going to stay on that humid train, jammed in like a sardine on the way to a job that sucks the life out of you every minute of the day? Are you going to tread water in the Dead Zone for another five years? Are you going to crawl though city traffic or are you going to tap into the greatness that's inside all of us and find out what you are really capable of?

As that old quote says: 'Come to the edge', He said. They said, 'We are afraid.' 'Come to the edge,' He said. They came. He pushed them… and they flew.

A Great Opportunity to the readers of this book...

1: 'The 7 Steps To Increase Your Wealth and Multiply Your Income'. A groundbreaking audio program that is literally PACKED with vital information and specific techniques on lifting the lid on your income ceiling. Normally this would be $95 – yours for free as a reader of this book.

2: PLUS – A $700 discount Coupon to Brendan Nichols 'The Entrepreneur's Million Dollar Secrets' Boot Camp. This powerful 2 day seminar has literally made past participants millions and millions of dollars.
   • The mistakes that the vast majority of entrepreneurs do that literally flushes money down the toilet and HOW TO PREVENT IT.
   • The essential steps you must use to make more money but actually work less hours!
   • The Scientific, Low Cost strategies that produce large cash profits.

3: PLUS – '3 Reasons People Sabotage Their Success (that very few people know about) and How to Change It'. Your mindset is vital to your success. These Powerful Secrets show you why people destroy their success. Don't fall victim to being blind-sided by a Mack truck.

This mini e-book will show you how to bypass these hidden mine fields and program yourself for success. **Value $47.00**

4: **PLUS another extra bonus – 'The Financial Rescue Package' e - book.** Financial Rescue is written for people who want to get out of debt and create financial success! This powerful little book covers the 5 important areas that you must know to create financial success. These 5 essential areas are the foundation that is used by every successful person. It also gives you 10 very effective tips to help you on the path to financial freedom.

5: **PLUS another extra bonus - 'Create a Stampede of New Business and Profits'.** The 10 rules of the successful entrepreneur. A powerful 10 day course on discovering the tools to turn yourself into a highly successful entrepreneur.

Go Now to www.RichesFromBusiness.com/FreeGift to download your free gifts.

Brendan Nichols
The Advanced Cash Generation System

- A complete CD set

- A manual of the transcripts

- AND a step by step 252 page 'turn key' coaching manual with ready to use templates you can immediately utilize.

Discover the Specific Strategies That Can Revolutionize Your Profits.

What's in this Incredible system?
It's Unlike ANYTHING out there. The Most Advanced System to Generate Real Profits and Massively Accelerate Your Success. Check this out:
While most marketing systems focus on one or two areas – such as how to be a great copywriter or how to get low cost advertising and publicity or how to attract clients and increase your profits – THIS system covers all of that and almost EVERY conceivable marketing strategy to massively accelerate your success and profits.

It has 77 action steps and templates that you can specifically apply to grab more profits, opportunities, clients and cash.
This has been 11 months in the making and endless hours to ensure you get the most comprehensive and advanced profit increasing system available.
It's for the entrepreneur who wants to know how to massively increase their success and profits.

Go now to www.RichesFromBusiness.com and click on 'products' in the navigation bar to find out more.

Brendan Nichols
How to Become a Wealth Magnet

Warning: Perhaps the most important information on attracting massive wealth in record time, you have ever read.

A complete Home Seminar System

'Discover the Little-Known Beliefs and Success Strategies That Can Create Stacks of Money and a Gigantic Financial Breakthrough!'

Learn more about this amazing system and Discover How You Can Massively Increase Your Ability to Make Money.

- Want to make a lot more money this year?

- Not stress about paying the bills?

- Fast track your financial freedom?

- Go on some dream vacations?

Go now to www.RichesFromBusiness.com and click on 'products' in the navigation bar to find out more.

Brendan Nichols
The Remarkable Power-Selling Formula

NEW – Breakthrough Method to Sell Any Product or Service!!

For the First Time Ever – Someone has finally cracked the code on the step-by-step formula YOU MUST USE in a Specific Sequence to make massive sales! This is Powerful, Income Generating, Advanced Information!

Compiled in a New Home Seminar System – 6 CDs, a complete home coaching manual, PLUS another manual that has the entire transcripts of the CDs. It's easy; just follow the coaching manual and the 'Ready to Use' Formulas!

I am going to share with you a profound sales formula that can catapult your ability to MASSIVELY MULTIPLY YOUR INCOME …

Go now to www.RichesFromBusiness.com and click on 'products' in the navigation bar to find out more.

BRENDAN NICHOLS

Known as the 'Millionaire Mentor' by his tens of thousands of grateful business clients around the world who have come to his seminars, this straight-talking entrepreneur is famous for cutting to the chase and showing you the fast track to wealth and success.

He actually did it in the REAL WORLD before he ever taught a single person – in two different, highly successful businesses.

In the 1980s he ran a massively successful project marketing company where every sales person in the business was in the top 1% of sales people in the country. He has shared the stage with the likes of Tom Hopkins and Robert Kiyosaki, and thousands of people from Australia, USA, NZ, China and Asia have attended his dynamic seminars. He is a bestselling author and has done over 100 media interviews and appeared in almost every major newspaper in Australia. Three-quarters of a million people watched his ABC television documentary on achieving success.

www.RichesFromBusiness.com